until unity

francis
chan

DAVID C COOK

transforming lives together

UNTIL UNITY
Published by David C Cook
4050 Lee Vance Drive
Colorado Springs, CO 80918 U.S.A.

Integrity Music Limited, a Division of David C Cook
Brighton, East Sussex BN1 2RE, England

The graphic circle C logo is a registered trademark of David C Cook.

Library of Congress Control Number 2020952209
ISBN 978-0-8307-8272-7
eISBN 978-0-8307-8273-4

The Team: Michael Covington, Kevin Kim, Mercy Gordon, Mark Beuving,
Stephanie Bennett, Judy Gillispie, James Hershberger, Susan Murdock
Lead Cover Designer: Julie Ip
Cover Designer: Mackey Saturday

Printed in the United States of America
First Edition 2021

1 2 3 4 5 6 7 8 9 10

012721-BETH

until unity

This book is dedicated to the followers
of Jesus from various denominations
who have forgiven me for my arrogance
and divisiveness over the years.

And he gave the apostles, the prophets, the evangelists, the shepherds and teachers, to equip the saints for the work of ministry, for building up the body of Christ, <u>until we all attain to the unity of the faith</u> and of the knowledge of the Son of God, to mature manhood, to the measure of the stature of the fullness of Christ, so that we may no longer be children, tossed to and fro by the waves and carried about by every wind of doctrine, by human cunning, by craftiness in deceitful schemes. Rather, speaking the truth in love, we are to grow up in every way into him who is the head, into Christ, from whom the whole body, joined and held together by every joint with which it is equipped, when each part is working properly, makes the body grow so that it builds itself up in love.

Ephesians 4:11–16

Contents

Acknowledgments   11

Introduction   13

Chapter 1: It's What the Trinity Wants   35

Chapter 2: It's What You Want   53

Chapter 3: It's What the World Needs   75

Chapter 4: It Starts with Repentance   97

Chapter 5: It Comes with Maturity   119

Chapter 6: It Survives with Love   137

Chapter 7: It Requires a Fight   161

Chapter 8: It Must Start Small   191

Conclusion: A Return to Childlike Faith   207

Notes   215

Scripture Index   217

Acknowledgments

Mercy: You're listed as editor, but you did much more. I couldn't have written this book without you. You are brilliant. Your wisdom coupled with your deep and pure love for Jesus made writing fun for me. There's no one on earth I would rather write with. It was great to think with you, pray with you, and just be with you. You're the best.

Mark Beuving: thanks for contributing to yet another book despite being in a busy season.

To my church family in Hong Kong: Lem, Diana, Allison, Christy, David, Lillian, Julie, Alan, Jen, Eugene, Telly, Francis, Iris, Douglas, Kelly, Ka Yuen, Wai Wai, Ah Wing, Barry,

YY, Josh, Grazia, Sailor, Circle, Brian, James, Ka Yin, Helen, Hawk, Lorraine, Kyle, Jimmy, Hilda, Silas, On, Chicken, June, Jackie, Mike, Camilla, Amanda, Emma, JoJo, Andy, Andrew, Eric, Esther, Ah Sun, Ethan, Lap Yin. Thanks for making 2020 the best year of my life!

My friends in HK for your faithful prayers and support: Jackie P., Agnes, Jason, Juliana, Brian, Angela, Chow Fai, Kabo, Richard, Linda, Hugo, Yuenyi, TH, Paula, KO, YK, Serena, Cynthia, Sydney, Peter, Susana, James, Kennedy, Peter, Eugene, Matt, Robert, Pinky, Ben, the Balcombe family, Matt and Rebekah.

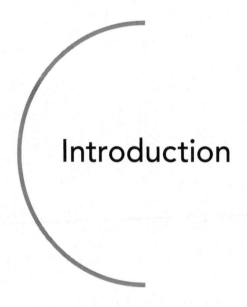

Introduction

Be honest: How much time did you spend praising Jesus this morning?

Asking for things doesn't count. Just reading a passage of Scripture doesn't count. I'm asking, How much time did you spend staring at Him and telling Him how amazing He is?

We were God's enemy, destined to face His wrath. Let that sink in.

Jesus was tortured on the cross to appease the wrath of God. Does that truth still move you?

You are now reconciled with God and adopted as His child. How do we go a day without praising Him for this?

There is nothing you have to
do today that is more important
than worshipping Him.

God now abides in you! Don't just give this a head nod. Marvel at this!

Put this book down and worship Him. You are breathing now because God is giving you breath. Use your next breath for its intended purpose. Bless Him.

> *Bless the LORD, O my soul,*
> *and all that is within me,*
> *bless his holy name!*
>
> —Psalm 103:1

We can't start our days without praise. We are commanded to rejoice in Him always. There is nothing you have to do today that is more important than worshipping Him. If I'm not wise enough to start my day with praise, why should anyone listen to what I have to say? If I am foolish enough to forego praise because my mind is needed to fix problems in the church, then I'm more of the problem than I realize.

Our lack of praise may actually be the biggest cause of our divisions. Once we stop worshipping, all hope for unity is lost. This is what unites us: we can't stop talking about the treasure we have in Jesus. It's hard to start an argument with someone who is on her knees shouting praises to Jesus, especially when you're busy blessing the Lord as well. Many of our problems could be reconciled if we discussed our concerns on our knees before a Holy God. We can't allow the Enemy or our enemies to interrupt our praise. Worship is our path to unity.

Even now I would encourage you to look up the following passages that explain the truths mentioned above: Romans 5:10–11; Ephesians 2:3–4; Romans 3:23–25; 1 John 3:1; 2 Corinthians 5:21; John 14:21–23. Fill your heart with worship, and keep it filled. You and I are part of an outrageous love story. Once we lose our fascination, we lose our effectiveness. Our words end up doing more harm than good. With a heart of thanksgiving, let's address the issues.

Our Broken Family

We are currently the most divided faith group on earth, and there isn't a close second. If you think I'm exaggerating, name another religion with more than two or three factions. We have thousands of denominations and ministries, each believing their theology or methodology is superior. The saddest part of this is that our Savior was crucified to end our divisions, commands us to be united, and says we will impact the world when we become one.

We can't just go back to our various circles and continue our discussions about how deceived our brothers and sisters are. It's time to try something different. What if we each made it our goal to strive for a level of humility we've never had? We could spend our circle time on our knees crying out to the God of truth, begging Him to expose any pride or deception that has crept into our own lives.

We need to stop thinking that our primary duty toward our fellow believers is to critique them. It's not. Our primary duty is to love them. Paul says we owe a debt of love to each other (Rom. 13:8). Yet it seems we invest far more time in learning than loving. Honestly evaluate the amount of time you spend acquiring information compared to the amount of time you spend asking God to increase your love for His children.

We have been treating our divisions like our national debt. It worsens every minute, but it doesn't affect our daily lives so we don't feel an urgency to change it. That's at the root of the problem: we can't stop thinking about ourselves. We have forgotten how our divisions affect God and an unbelieving world. Our casual, dismissive attitude toward unity is incredibly dangerous for three reasons:

1. God is disgusted with it.
2. The world is confused by it.
3. It could be evidence that the Holy Spirit is not in us.

Tremble

I don't want this book to be my efforts at talking you out of division. That won't last. The wisdom to refrain from unloving speech has to start with a fear of God and His commands. In Isaiah 66, God says:

> *Thus says the LORD:*
> *"Heaven is my throne,*
> *and the earth is my footstool;*
> *what is the house that you would build for me,*
> *and what is the place of my rest?*
> *All these things my hand has made,*
> *and so all these things came to be,*
> *declares the LORD.*
> *But this is the one to whom I will look:*
> *he who is humble and contrite in spirit*
> *and trembles at my word."* (vv. 1–2)

Whom does God look to? The humble person who *trembles at His word!*

You're about to read through some Scriptures regarding unity. Before you do so, take a moment to remember that these Scriptures are sacred commands from a terrifying God. Some of you may have been taught to tremble at commands regarding sexual immorality but not the ones demanding unity. Unity has been looked at as a cute topic for those who don't have the theological expertise to look into deeper issues. Unity has been viewed as a soft option for those who don't care about truth. I urge you to let go of any of that mentality and simply tremble at each verse before a Holy God. Only when we take Scripture seriously will we understand that God cares more about unity than any human being ever has.

I am convinced that if you tremble at these Scriptures, you won't even have to read the rest of the book. I pray that God would choose to pour His grace out as you read His commands. I would love to hear from readers, "I never got past the introduction. It was all I needed."

> *There are six things that the LORD hates,*
> *seven that are an abomination to him:*
> *haughty eyes, a lying tongue,*
> *and hands that shed innocent blood,*
> *a heart that devises wicked plans,*
> *feet that make haste to run to evil,*
> *a false witness who breathes out lies,*
> *and one who sows discord among brothers.*
> —Proverbs 6:16–19

> *I do not ask for these only, but also for those*
> *who will believe in me through their word,*
> *that they may all be one, just as you, Father,*
> *are in me, and I in you, that they also may be*
> *in us, so that the world may believe that you*
> *have sent me. The glory that you have given*
> *me I have given to them, that they may be one*

even as we are one, I in them and you in me,
that they may become perfectly one, so that the
world may know that you sent me and loved
them even as you loved me.

—John 17:20–23

I therefore, a prisoner for the Lord, urge you
to walk in a manner worthy of the calling to
which you have been called, with all humility
and gentleness, with patience, bearing with one
another in love, eager to maintain the unity of
the Spirit in the bond of peace. There is one body
and one Spirit—just as you were called to the
one hope that belongs to your call—one Lord,
one faith, one baptism, one God and Father of
all, who is over all and through all and in all.

—Ephesians 4:1–6

But avoid foolish controversies, genealogies, dis-
sensions, and quarrels about the law, for they
are unprofitable and worthless. As for a person
who stirs up division, after warning him once
and then twice, have nothing more to do with
him, knowing that such a person is warped and
sinful; he is self-condemned.

—Titus 3:9–11

*For as many of you as were baptized into Christ
have put on Christ. There is neither Jew nor Greek,
there is neither slave nor free, there is no male and
female, for you are all one in Christ Jesus.*

—Galatians 3:27–28

*Who are you to pass judgment on the servant
of another? It is before his own master that he
stands or falls. And he will be upheld, for the
Lord is able to make him stand.*

—Romans 14:4

*I appeal to you, brothers, by the name of our
Lord Jesus Christ, that all of you agree, and
that there be no divisions among you, but that
you be united in the same mind and the same
judgment.*

—1 Corinthians 1:10

*So if there is any encouragement in Christ,
any comfort from love, any participation in
the Spirit, any affection and sympathy, complete my joy by being of the same mind, having
the same love, being in full accord and of one
mind.*

—Philippians 2:1–2

Therefore let no one pass judgment on you in questions of food and drink, or with regard to a festival or a new moon or a Sabbath. These are a shadow of the things to come, but the substance belongs to Christ. Let no one disqualify you, insisting on asceticism and worship of angels, going on in detail about visions, puffed up without reason by his sensuous mind, and not holding fast to the Head, from whom the whole body, nourished and knit together through its joints and ligaments, grows with a growth that is from God.

—Colossians 2:16–19

Now may our God and Father himself, and our Lord Jesus, direct our way to you, and may the Lord make you increase and abound in love for one another and for all, as we do for you, so that he may establish your hearts blameless in holiness before our God and Father, at the coming of our Lord Jesus with all his saints.

—1 Thessalonians 3:11–13

The aim of our charge is love that issues from a pure heart and a good conscience and a sincere faith. Certain persons, by swerving from these, have wandered away into vain discussion, desiring to be teachers of the law, without understanding either what they are saying or the things about which they make confident assertions.

—1 Timothy 1:5–7

If anyone teaches a different doctrine and does not agree with the sound words of our Lord Jesus Christ and the teaching that accords with godliness, he is puffed up with conceit and understands nothing. He has an unhealthy craving for controversy and for quarrels about words, which produce envy, dissension, slander, evil suspicions, and constant friction among people who are depraved in mind and deprived of the truth, imagining that godliness is a means of gain.

—1 Timothy 6:3–5

Have nothing to do with foolish, ignorant controversies; you know that they breed quarrels. And the Lord's servant must not be quarrelsome but kind to everyone, able to teach, patiently enduring evil, correcting his opponents with gentleness.

—2 Timothy 2:23–25

But the wisdom from above is first pure, then peaceable, gentle, open to reason, full of mercy and good fruits, impartial and sincere. And a harvest of righteousness is sown in peace by those who make peace.

—James 3:17–18

Whoever says he is in the light and hates his brother is still in darkness. Whoever loves his brother abides in the light, and in him there is no cause for stumbling. But whoever hates his brother is in the darkness and walks in the darkness, and does not know where he is going, because the darkness has blinded his eyes.

—1 John 2:9–11

In this is love, not that we have loved God but that he loved us and sent his Son to be the propitiation for our sins. Beloved, if God so loved us, we also ought to love one another. No one has ever seen God; if we love one another, God abides in us and his love is perfected in us.

—1 John 4:10–12

> *Blessed are the peacemakers, for they shall be*
> *called sons of God.*
>
> —Matthew 5:9

Please don't be afraid to take these commands literally. It has become the case that if I take a biblical statement about sexual behavior literally, I'm called a conservative and my stance is considered "biblical." But, sadly, if I take one of these biblical statements about avoiding disunity or pursuing oneness literally, I'm called a liberal and my stance is considered soft and cowardly and compromising.

That's wrong. We all have to make choices about which parts of the Bible are meant to be taken literally. All of us. I can't tell you every passage that is meant to be taken purely literally. (Selling all your possessions? Plucking out your eye? Wearing head coverings?) But I can tell you that I'm extremely confident that Jesus' commands to love and be unified and to avoid controversy are meant to be taken literally.

Witness

Have you ever considered how outsiders must view us? Try to imagine an unbeliever going online and trying to make sense of all the different denominations, church splits, competitive advertising, and open slander. It would look like my family screaming frantically at each other while walking through an orphanage to meet kids wanting adoption. There is a reason people aren't anxious to join our family. What picture of God are we showing to the world? If the church is supposed to be a reflection of the image of God and the aroma of Christ to those who are perishing, it is no wonder that people are not attracted. Don't try to comfort yourself with verses like John 15:18: "If the world hates you, know that it has hated me before it hated you." The world currently hates us not because we resemble Jesus but because we don't. We are arrogant and there is a serious disconnect between our beliefs and actions.

Scripture teaches that our influence on the world is directly tied to the unity we display. Meanwhile, we continue to publicly degrade one another, oblivious to how we appear to the world. We continue to draw lines that make sense to *us* but not to those watching. Does this bother you? Don't forget that we are talking about real people headed for a real Hell. Don't just lump everyone into some vague group. We are talking about your friends, cousins, children, and neighbors. They are all glad that Christianity works for you, but they don't see any need to be "saved" by Jesus. They don't even believe in a Judgment Day. According to Scripture, that would change if the Church were united.

Scripture teaches that our influence on the world is directly tied to the unity we display.

> *Only let your manner of life be worthy of the*
> *gospel of Christ, so that whether I come and see*
> *you or am absent, I may hear of you that you are*
> *standing firm in one spirit, with one mind striv-*
> *ing side by side for the faith of the gospel, and not*
> *frightened in anything by your opponents. This*
> *is a clear sign to them of their destruction, but of*
> *your salvation, and that from God.*
> —Philippians 1:27–28

It's great that you share the gospel with those you love, but it's our unity that will cause them to actually believe your words. Most of us would say that we would do anything to see our loved ones know Jesus. Are you willing to make a serious effort toward unity? How much humbling, repentance, and suffering are you willing to endure to see the Church unified?

Salvation

If you find yourself apathetic toward the commands of God for unity and unconcerned with how this appears to the world, you might have a bigger problem. It's possible that the Holy Spirit is not in you, that you are not really saved. Does that sound like a shocking statement? It shouldn't. Scripture is clear about the marks of a true believer and the fruit that flows out of a life indwelt by the Holy Spirit:

Now the works of the flesh are evident: sexual immorality, impurity, sensuality, idolatry, sorcery, enmity, strife, jealousy, fits of anger, rivalries, dissensions, divisions, envy, drunkenness, orgies, and things like these. I warn you, as I warned you before, that those who do such things will not inherit the kingdom of God. But the fruit of the Spirit is love, joy, peace, patience, kindness, goodness, faithfulness, gentleness, self-control; against such things there is no law.

—Galatians 5:19–23

I want you to take a close look at the first list: the works of the flesh. It's easy to glance over it and check off enough boxes to assure ourselves we have nothing to worry about. I'm not living in sexual immorality or drunkenness, and I've never thought about becoming a sorcerer, so I'm good. But have you ever noticed that enmity, strife, jealousy, anger, rivalry, dissension, division, and envy are also on that list? And have you ever really trembled at the warning that "those who do such things **will not inherit the kingdom of God**"? God takes these sins seriously, much more seriously than we do in the modern church, and if we do not change, we will reap the consequences.

Now look at that second list—the one you probably have memorized:

> *But the fruit of the Spirit is love, joy, peace,*
> *patience, kindness, goodness, faithfulness, gentle-*
> *ness, self-control; against such things there is*
> *no law.*
>
> —Galatians 5:22–23

I think this is a good time to remind you that just because you believe a truth doesn't guarantee you possess it. "A. W. Tozer describes the textualist as a person who assumes that because he affirms the Bible's veracity, he automatically possesses the things of which the Bible speaks."[1] Too many people live as though affirming a biblical truth is equivalent to having it in reality. Seminary can teach you how to memorize a menu, but that doesn't ensure you'll ever taste the food. It's terrifying to think that Hell may have no shortage of Bible teachers with good theology.

Back to Galatians: Paul is explaining the fruit that results from a person rooted in the Spirit. Don't treat this as I used to—a checklist to find my weaknesses so I can work on those areas. The point is that a good tree will produce good fruit. This is what the Spirit *will* produce when He becomes the new master of a person. Don't get caught up in working harder to change the fruit of your life. Get to the root. Why do words come out of your mouth that sound unkind, ungentle, unloving? Jesus says the problem is not your mouth but your heart (Matt. 12:34). If love, joy, peace, patience, kindness, goodness, faithfulness, gentleness, and self-control are not flowing out of our hearts, it's not because we aren't trying hard enough. It's because we're not connected to the Spirit of God. It's that serious.

End the Hopelessness

The situation that the Christian Church finds itself in appears hopeless. We have tried holding events to promote unity, creating common doctrinal statements to build unity, and even praying for unity. Nothing has worked because we are not getting to the root issue. We think the problem is differences in theology or practice, so we spend a lot of time arguing about different passages in Scripture. We believe unity will only happen once we convert the other side to our opinion.

In reality, our divisions are caused by much deeper issues: our conflicting desires (James 4), our propensity for jealousy and selfish ambition, which leads to "disorder and every vile practice" (James 3), and ultimately the immaturity of our faith. Too many people call themselves Christian who have never experienced a deep connection with God. Because so few people have experienced His love, even fewer are able to share it. If our relationship with God is robotic or nonexistent, our bond of love with others will be equally weak. When love is shallow, all it takes is something as trivial as a disagreement to divide us.

I know I will be mocked for my simplicity, but love really is the answer. Somehow, as we have advanced in our sophisticated theological discussions, we have stopped growing in our love for God and each other. Yet Jesus said that love for God and love for our neighbor are literally the most important things (Mark 12:28–31). There is a hope for unity, but until you are willing to accept the simplicity of it, we will continue to divide.

A miracle was supposed to happen when the Holy Spirit entered our bodies: we were supposed to yield the fruit of supernatural love for each other. It didn't happen. In fact, the opposite did. If there truly is one unity-loving Spirit leading us, it makes no sense that we are becoming more and more divided. So either the Spirit never entered some of us, or we have done a masterful job of suppressing Him. No matter how many Bible verses you know and how well you can teach the Scriptures, you have to be willing to examine the fruit of your life to see if the Spirit has truly entered you.

After honest examination, you may discover that you are not as humble and loving as you thought. If you don't really love people that deeply, it could be because you haven't experienced the love of Christ deeply. There may be an arrogance or emptiness in your soul that has caused more division than you realize. It might not be everyone else's fault after all. Will you humble yourself to admit the possibility of pride in your life that requires repentance? This could turn out to be the greatest discovery of your life. Humility and repentance always lead to life and grace. It could be that repenting of our pride will lead to a vibrant love relationship with God and others, resulting in a fullness of life that we've never tasted.

> *Put on then, as God's chosen ones, holy and beloved, compassionate hearts, kindness, humility, meekness, and patience, bearing with one another and, if one has a complaint against another, forgiving each other; as the Lord has forgiven you, so you also must forgive. And above all these put on love, which binds everything together in perfect harmony. And let the peace of Christ rule in your hearts, to which indeed you were called in one body.*
>
> —Colossians 3:12–15

Throughout the Scriptures, we see God place people in seemingly impossible situations. He then moves miraculously to display His power (e.g., parting the Red Sea, raising Lazarus from the dead, etc.). As our divisions increase and deepen, we find ourselves again in a situation that requires a miracle. Now seems to be the perfect time for God to answer the prayer that Christ prayed for oneness (John 17). While some people in the church add to the division, I believe there is a much greater army of believers who are done with all the needless fights and factions. There are swarms of saints on their knees praying like Christ that we would become one. There are men and women with childlike faith who are willing to pay the price to fight for unity. Most importantly, we have a God who performed the most loving act in history because He wanted us to be one with Him. Why wouldn't we believe that He would move now to make His children one with each other?

Chapter 1

It's What the Trinity Wants

"Let us make man in our image, after our likeness."

What comes to mind when you read those words from Genesis 1:26? Have you ever meditated on this? It is one of those verses I had known for years but never really explored. As a result, I never thought about what an outrageous honor it is to be created in the likeness of God! I spent many hours fixated on my own sin and weaknesses, but I never took time to marvel at being made like Him.

Most Bible teachers agree that "us" and "our" are used because God is speaking as a Trinity. Genesis 1:2 explains that the Spirit was present at creation. John 1:1–3 tells us that

Jesus was active in creating all things. In a sacred moment, God says, "Let us make man in our image." I would encourage you to literally spend hours just meditating on this single phrase. Even now, I strongly urge you to spend a few minutes meditating on it after begging Him to enlighten you. The rest of the book can wait. In fact, the rest of this book will make much more sense if you allow the Holy Spirit to take you into a deep meditation of this verse.

When was the last time you heard someone express fascination over being created in His image? James warns us to be careful how we speak to the people around us because those people are made in God's image: "No human being can tame the tongue. It is a restless evil, full of deadly poison. With it we bless our Lord and Father, and with it we curse people who are made in the likeness of God. From the same mouth come blessing and cursing. My brothers, these things ought not to be so" (James 3:8–10).

We are made in the image of God! Most people know that it's true but don't realize that it's sacred. Thinking only in the physical, they might picture God looking like a larger version of themselves. That's what the Greeks did with their gods and demigods. Is that really what the Bible is talking about here? I think we would all agree that it goes far deeper than physical appearance. Jesus explained to a woman from Samaria that "God is spirit, and those who worship him must worship in spirit and truth" (John 4:24). What does it mean to be made in the image of a God who is spirit? While being created in His image may involve something physical, it seems more likely that being His image bearers has more to do with things we cannot see.

Created in the Image of the Trinity

Assuming you believe in the Trinity, have you ever thought about the implications of being created in the image of one God who exists as three Persons? We have a God who exists eternally in *perfect relationship*. What does that mean for us as people made in His image? We want to be careful not to speculate about something so sacred, but Jesus gives us quite a bit of insight in John 14–17. It seems we were created in such a way that we are capable of attaining oneness with God and each other.

Jesus explains to Philip that anyone who has seen Him has seen His Father (14:9). This is one of the most confusing claims in history. It's a concept with no earthly parallel, so it sounds contradictory. To confuse matters even more, Jesus tells the disciples that He will send another Counselor who will actually reside "in" them (vv. 16–17). This whole discourse from Jesus stretches our minds and forces us to see ourselves as more than just physical beings. In verse 23, He tells us that He and the Father will make Their home in us. In 15:4, Jesus tells us to live in Him and He will live in us. In John 17:20–23, He says the following:

> *I do not ask for these only, but also for those who will believe in me through their word, that they may all be one, just as you, Father, are in me, and I in you, that they also may be in us, so that the world may believe that you have sent me. The glory that you have given me I have given to them, that they may be one even as we are one, I in them and you in me, that they may become perfectly one, so that the world may know that you sent me and loved them even as you loved me.*

In some real way, I am currently in Jesus, the Spirit is in me, and the Father and Son make Their home in me. Did you take that in? It's an insane statement that would be blasphemous if it didn't come from God's own words! In addition to that, Jesus' prayer is that every believer will join in this same perfect oneness that the Father, Son, and Holy Spirit have enjoyed for all eternity. We were created in His image, so we can join in this unity.

We need to spend more time meditating on mysteries like this. It is true that God "dwells in unapproachable light, whom no one has ever seen or can see" (1 Tim. 6:16), and yet we can live in Him as He lives in us. Somehow we can be "filled with all the fullness of God" (Eph. 3:19), and "become partakers of the divine nature" (2 Peter 1:4). These statements do not come from a human desire to make ourselves like God—these are God's statements about us! Sit in silence and ask God to give you a glimpse of what He means in those verses.

We are invited into something deeper than what the Israelites experienced (Ex. 19:16–20). They stood at the base of the mountain and watched Moses ascend into the presence of God. Moses had the honor of speaking to God and hearing God answer him in thunder. As mind-blowing as that scene is, we are invited into something deeper. We are not just standing on the outside and staring at a Person in adoration. He calls us to actually enter Him, be filled with Him, and partake of Him. We were created in such a way that this is possible. Belief in the atoning death of Christ recreates us to make this a reality (2 Cor. 5:17). His desire is to be perfectly one with you, but not just you. The prayer of Christ is that His creation would enjoy what they were created for—a perfect unity between Father, Son, Holy Spirit, and all whom Jesus saved.

We worship a God who desires
unity with His children *and*
between His children.

The Father Who Hates Division

He yearns jealously over the spirit that he has made to dwell in us.

—James 4:5

This is another one of those verses that requires deep prayer and meditation to comprehend. It takes tremendous faith to believe that Almighty God could have such a strong desire for us. Do you believe that you have a heavenly Father who "yearns jealously" for you? He created Adam and Eve to walk with Him in the garden, and He created us to not only walk *with* Him but *in* Him. He yearns jealously for this.

Parents might get a small taste of God's emotions with their own children. You produce a life, knowing that the baby will one day have the freedom to ignore you and live independently if he or she chooses. Everything in you hopes this child will want to stay connected. Part of you wants to demand it because you want it so badly, but you know that isn't love. The heartbreak parents feel when their child wants to live independent of them is a fraction of what the Creator feels. Imagine how He feels knowing that some of His children wish He didn't exist. They're busy and tired of trying to squeeze in a token visit as their duty. Their desire to ignore Him is so strong that they convince themselves He's not real. Romans 1 explains that though they know

He exists, they suppress the truth. That's how badly they want freedom from Him.

We worship a God who desires unity with His children *and* between His children. He sent His Son to bring His children together under His care. No good father wants to see separation between his children. As a father of seven, it would crush me to see any of my children rejected and separated from the others. It would anger me to see any of my children being divisive. In God's list of things He hates (Prov. 6:16–19), He places greatest emphasis on "one who sows discord among brothers." He calls it an "abomination"! That should stop you dead in your tracks. You should be examining your own life right now to see if you are guilty of something that Almighty God hates so much. If you can casually read on to the next paragraph, you have a serious problem.

I am guilty of having sowed discord. Even now, as I study all these passages about division, I am embarrassed by my lack of remorse. Only a redemptive God with grace beyond comprehension could be this patient with me and still use me to teach about unity. I have spent most of my Christian life wishing that certain pockets of Christians did not exist. I even had the audacity to pray for the deaths of certain people because I thought their removal would benefit His Kingdom on earth. I was not just a run-of-the-mill arrogant person.

That's next-level stuff! Think about the pride it requires to come before an omniscient God to share that kind of idea.

I was too quick to label people as false teachers, warning believers to keep their distance from them. While there is a time to warn others about false teachers, there is also a time to do your homework. By being too quick to judge, I have made costly mistakes. I jumped on bandwagons that were popular in my theological circle, attacking men and women whom I now know to be God's beloved children.

Proverbs paints this as more than a "mistake." All of that was an "abomination" to Him.

Maybe I was cunning enough to refrain from openly slandering them in public, but I'm sure my heart attitude spilled out of my mouth. None of us are as good at faking love as we think. Besides, just because my statements weren't made in public doesn't mean God hated it less. Every unkind word spoken in private about one of His children was heard by Him. It really wasn't private, and I doubt I would have said those things if I had been aware of their Dad's presence in the room. Sometimes the secret conversations are the most dangerous. They seed deeper-rooted division in a person, who then passes on the slander. That's unholy discipleship. God hates it.

Praise God for the cross! Now would be a fitting time to worship Him for His mercy. All of my abominable acts were placed on Jesus at the cross. Jesus died to pay for our divisiveness and to lead us toward unity.

The Son Who Died to Bring Us Together

How can so many of us miss the importance of unity when it's the whole point of the cross? Jesus suffered and died to unite us with the Father and with each other. To disregard unity is to disparage the cross. In speaking about the way the Romans ate controversial foods without considering how it affected their fellow believers, Paul says that these Christians were actually "destroy[ing] the one for whom Christ died" (Rom. 14:15). He couldn't have stated it more strongly! It draws on the same truth he explains in great detail in Ephesians:

> *But now in Christ Jesus you who once were far off have been brought near by the blood of Christ. For he himself is our peace, who has made us both one and has broken down in his flesh the dividing wall of hostility by abolishing the law of commandments expressed in ordinances, that he might create in himself one new man in place of the two, so making peace, and might reconcile us both to God in*

*one body through the cross, thereby killing the
hostility. And he came and preached peace to
you who were far off and peace to those who
were near. For through him we both have
access in one Spirit to the Father. So then you
are no longer strangers and aliens, but you are
fellow citizens with the saints and members of
the household of God, built on the foundation
of the apostles and prophets, Christ Jesus himself being the cornerstone, in whom the whole
structure, being joined together, grows into a
holy temple in the Lord. In him you also are
being built together into a dwelling place for
God by the Spirit.*

—Ephesians 2:13–22

Everyone in Heaven stares at Jesus in awe. Thousands of years after first believing, they continue to marvel at Him. "Worthy is the Lamb who was slain" (Rev. 5:12). People who once hated each other are praising in unison. One sacred act brings them to their knees in adoration, where they find themselves kneeling beside those they used to dislike.

I find myself writing and deleting, writing and deleting, in this section. It's because there's nothing to add to Ephesians 2:13–22. There isn't anything confusing in the passage that needs explaining. It says it all. Please read it again slowly and prayerfully. It is supernatural and should lead you into a time of deep praise and repentance.

The Spirit Who Grieves Our Divisions

Most Christians know that the Holy Spirit is a Person, but they still tend to treat Him like an impersonal force. We have a lot of discussions about what He does and does not do, lots of debates about what the Scriptures say about Him. I find that one thing is missing from most of these discussions about the Holy Spirit: fear.

Think back to the last few times you spoke about the Holy Spirit. Was there a reverence in your tone as you dared speak about a God who is far more powerful than you can imagine? Did you speak with a humility that showed that His ways were far beyond your comprehension? I am so embarrassed about having partaken in casual and even arrogant debates about Him. I have spoken about Him as though I were some kind of expert on Him. Think about the level of pride and ignorance required for a human being to think he could speak as an expert on the Holy Spirit. It's absolutely ridiculous! Thank you, Lord, for your mercy.

From the throne came flashes of lightning, and rumblings and peals of thunder, and before the

throne were burning seven torches of fire, which
are the seven spirits of God.

—Revelation 4:5

I have no idea what it will be like the first time I see Jesus, and I'm completely clueless as to what my first encounter with the Holy Spirit will be like. To even try to imagine it feels like we are walking on holy ground. It is sacred to speak about Him.

I remember the first time I read that the Holy Spirit could be grieved (Eph. 4:30). I was confused. I was one of those people who didn't treat the Holy Spirit as a Person, even though I knew theologically that He is. Even in the times I was fully aware of His Personhood, I assumed that His infinite power precluded Him from grieving. Scripture refutes that.

Let no corrupting talk come out of your mouths,
but only such as is good for building up, as fits
the occasion, that it may give grace to those who
hear. And do not grieve the Holy Spirit of God,
by whom you were sealed for the day of redemp-
tion. Let all bitterness and wrath and anger
and clamor and slander be put away from you,
along with all malice.

—Ephesians 4:29–31

Jesus died to pay for our
divisiveness and to lead
us toward unity.

The Holy Spirit grieves, and Paul speaks of His grieving in the context of our divisive words and actions. Have you ever thought seriously about the truth that your words could grieve a Holy God? This should affect us deeply.

If the Spirit is grieved and the Spirit dwells in me, I would be feeling that grief. You can't separate it and say, "Well, the Spirit is grieved but I'm fine. I have thicker skin."

There's a serious problem if the Spirit is grieving our division yet we feel fine about it.

Help Me Feel What You Feel

It is only recently that the Lord has given me wisdom to pray, "Help me feel what You feel." I saw so many instances in Scripture where godly people felt what God felt and ungodly ones did not. God has never been a God who merely wanted us to intellectually believe truths and begrudgingly obey commands. He wants true love—the kind of love where you become so perfectly one that you begin to feel what He feels. In fact, this is one of the reasons the Spirit dwells in us. His indwelling creates an inseparable oneness. The more your spirit gets intertwined with His, the more you will feel what He feels, love what He loves, grieve over what grieves Him.

Oddly, Ezekiel 9:4 and Revelation 9:4 both speak about God marking the foreheads of His people so they are protected from the judgments that will fall on the rest of mankind. This is similar to what happened in Egypt when the destroying angel passed over the homes sealed with the blood of the lamb. We need to pay attention to these patterns in the actions of God. Notice how Ezekiel describes those who were sealed:

> And the LORD said to him, "Pass through the city, through Jerusalem, and put a mark on the foreheads of the men who sigh and groan over all the abominations that are committed in it." And to the others he said in my hearing, "Pass through the city after him, and strike. Your eye shall not spare, and you shall show no pity. Kill old men outright, young men and maidens, little children and women, but touch no one on whom is the mark. And begin at my sanctuary." So they began with the elders who were before the house.
>
> —Ezekiel 9:4–6

The ones who escaped the wrath of God were those who "sigh and groan over all the abominations that are committed in it." The seal was reserved for those whose hearts matched God's in sighing and groaning over the sins surrounding them.

Lot was an interesting character in the Old Testament, but Peter speaks of his soul being grieved as well:

> *[God] rescued righteous Lot, greatly distressed*
> *by the sensual conduct of the wicked (for as that*
> *righteous man lived among them day after day,*
> *he was tormenting his righteous soul over their*
> *lawless deeds that he saw and heard)....*
>
> —2 Peter 2:7–8

He was "greatly distressed" by the sin of the world around him. His "righteous soul" was "torment[ed]." We spend our days in a very ungodly time. We can't allow our souls to become indifferent or calloused to the evil around us. Though it is easier to ignore what's going on in the world, God was pleased with Lot because he allowed his soul to be tormented. He felt what God felt.

Follow me on this a bit longer. God commanded Ezekiel to groan "with breaking heart and bitter grief" over what was happening to His people (21:6). Through the prophet Zephaniah, God promised to gather the remnant of His people who mourned over the wickedness of the earth (3:18). In Revelation, He praised the church in Ephesus because "you hate the works of the Nicolaitans, which I also hate" (2:2–6). Nehemiah wept over the ruin of God's city and people (Neh. 1:4; 2:2–3), and David "shed streams of tears" because people were not keeping God's law (Ps. 119:136). At the conclusion of the book of Jonah, God confronted His reluctant prophet because he was unwilling to share the pity that God had for the wayward nation of Nineveh (4:10–11). Amos rebuked the people for enjoying themselves but refusing to grieve over the ruin of God's people (6:4–6).

Sometimes when Lisa and I watch a movie together, we have very different reactions. It's jarring to be totally bored by a movie and then to look over at Lisa and see that she's crying her eyes out!

I believe something like this often happens between Christ and His Bride. God has told us what He cares about most. He's spelled out for us the things that actually cause Him grief, that make Him weep. And yet here we are, disregarding the unity His Son gave His life to secure and attacking each other over things that are irrelevant! This scenario happens all the time. The things that bother us are not the things that bother God. Meanwhile, He is disturbed by things to which we seem indifferent.

God, help us feel what You feel. Align our desires with Yours.

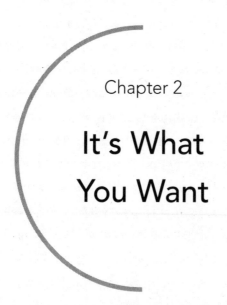

Chapter 2

It's What You Want

We've all watched videos showing the tininess of the Earth in comparison to the sun, stars, solar system, galaxy, galaxies … Now imagine one Being opening His mouth and causing all of that to appear instantaneously. Close your eyes right now and try to fathom the power of that moment.

Now imagine that Being entering your body.

That is what happens at the moment of true belief. Many of you have been fooled into believing that salvation is a mere moment when you affirm the crucifixion and resurrection, resulting in your escape from God's wrath. If that's you, then you have missed the point of the New Testament. Being born again is not just a one-time transaction and then waiting for death to experience the results. It is about experiencing the life of God here and now.

A God who slips into a person without causing any noticeable effect does not sound like a God worth worshipping. That doesn't describe the God I read about in Scripture. On the contrary, I worship a God whose resurrection power brings the dead to life and puts to death those things that repulse Him.

> *… and what is the immeasurable greatness of his power toward us who believe, according to the working of his great might that he worked in Christ when he raised him from the dead and seated him at his right hand in the heavenly places, far above all rule and authority and power and dominion, and above every name that is named, not only in this age but also in the one to come. And he put all things under his feet and gave him as head over all things to the church, which is his body, the fullness of him who fills all in all.*
>
> —Ephesians 1:19–23

> *If the Spirit of him who raised Jesus from the dead dwells in you, he who raised Christ Jesus*

*from the dead will also give life to your mortal
bodies through his Spirit who dwells in you. So
then, brothers, we are debtors, not to the flesh,
to live according to the flesh. For if you live
according to the flesh you will die, but if by the
Spirit you put to death the deeds of the body,
you will live. For all who are led by the Spirit of
God are sons of God.*

—Romans 8:11–14

I hope that everything inside of you is overflowing with
excitement. I pray these verses enable you to walk around
with confidence, assured that you have resurrection power to
overcome anything. Peter tells us that we become "partakers
of the divine nature" (2 Peter 1:4). Soak that in.

We are led by a God who desires unity! This is the
reason true believers are prone to unify. We share a common miracle. We were weak and dead; then everything
changed. We experience a grace that leaves us speechless.
Imagine you and a random stranger are cowering in pain
because you contracted a deadly disease. Now you are
blind, screaming in agony, and on the brink of death. A
man walks up to you both and miraculously heals you,
restores your sight, and hands you each a billion dollars.
Imagine the look you would give each other as you receive
the gift. That's the expression of shock that should bind

believers together. We should be staring at each other with a look that says, "What in the world just happened to us? We went from enemies of God to children of God! Our eternal destiny just changed! AND THE LIVING GOD JUST ENTERED OUR BODIES!"

Why don't Christians look at each other with that look? Could it be possible we haven't experienced this miracle? If we had, wouldn't we be so overjoyed by this that we would hardly notice our differences?

Inevitable Division

> *For, in the first place, when you come together as a church, I hear that there are divisions among you. And I believe it in part, for there must be factions among you in order that those who are genuine among you may be recognized.*
> —1 Corinthians 11:18–19

Paul tells the Corinthians that division in their case was inevitable because some of them were fake. The genuine believers were bound to stand out. The apostle John also speaks to this. He explains that some divisions happen because not everyone who attends our gatherings is truly part of us. "They went out from us, but they were not of us; for

if they had been of us, they would have continued with us"
(1 John 2:19). Throughout the letter, John warns that anyone
who claims to be Christian but shows no change of behavior
is a liar. These verses should terrify anyone who has felt secure
in a faith that produces no works. Read the following verses
with this question in mind: When a person experiences salvation, should we expect his or her life to change?

> *If we say we have fellowship with him while
> we walk in darkness, we lie and do not prac-
> tice the truth.*
>
> —1 John 1:6

> *And by this we know that we have come to know
> him, if we keep his commandments. Whoever
> says "I know him" but does not keep his com-
> mandments is a liar, and the truth is not in him,
> but whoever keeps his word, in him truly the love
> of God is perfected. By this we may know that we
> are in him: whoever says he abides in him ought
> to walk in the same way in which he walked.*
>
> —1 John 2:3-6

> *Whoever says he is in the light and hates his
> brother is still in darkness. Whoever loves his*

*brother abides in the light, and in him there is
no cause for stumbling.*

—1 John 2:9–10

*No one who abides in him keeps on sinning; no
one who keeps on sinning has either seen him or
known him.... By this it is evident who are the
children of God, and who are the children of
the devil: whoever does not practice righteousness is not of God, nor is the one who does not
love his brother.*

—1 John 3:6, 10

*We know that we have passed out of death into
life, because we love the brothers. Whoever does
not love abides in death. Everyone who hates his
brother is a murderer, and you know that no
murderer has eternal life abiding in him.*

—1 John 3:14–15

*But if anyone has the world's goods and sees
his brother in need, yet closes his heart against
him, how does God's love abide in him? Little
children, let us not love in word or talk but in
deed and in truth.*

—1 John 3:17–18

Beloved, let us love one another, for love is from God, and whoever loves has been born of God and knows God. Anyone who does not love does not know God, because God is love.

—1 John 4:7–8

We love because he first loved us. If anyone says, "I love God," and hates his brother, he is a liar; for he who does not love his brother whom he has seen cannot love God whom he has not seen. And this commandment we have from him: whoever loves God must also love his brother.

—1 John 4:19–21

By this we know that we love the children of God, when we love God and obey his commandments. For this is the love of God, that we keep his commandments. And his commandments are not burdensome.

—1 John 5:2–3

John uses stark language to make a simple but vital point: Being a Christian is not about making a claim about which religion you subscribe to. Being a Christian means that Christ has entered you, filled you with His love, and is

Being a Christian means
that Christ has entered you,
filled you with His love, and is
pouring His life through you
to the people around you.

pouring His life through you to the people around you. If you have experienced the life-changing love of Jesus, you will be overflowing with love for God and others. It's that simple. If you are prone to division and disunity, if you're having a hard time loving your brothers and sisters, then you have to ask the question: Has His Spirit really entered me?

If these passages create insecurity in you, don't just move on. Pick up your Bible and read the book of 1 John. You can read the entire book in less than ten minutes. John explains that he wrote these words so that true unity could happen (1 John 1:3). These words were meant to bring joy and an assurance of our salvation. If they bring concern and doubt, I am praying that everything would change as you read.

The worst thing you could do is become defensive at this point. It would be foolish to explain why John is wrong and your salvation was real despite the lack of change in your life. We are talking about the difference between eternity in Heaven or Hell. Even the most arrogant person should be jolted into honest examination by the severity of this. You may remember the moment of your "conversion"—the tears, the emotions. You remember the counselor guaranteeing that your profession of faith was proof of your faith. My experience was the same. I'm not saying it wasn't real. I am saying that if it was real, John claims that subsequent life change would result as well.

Being Assured of Your Salvation

I remember praying some version of the "sinner's prayer." Though that prayer is not found anywhere in Scripture, it's not wrong to pray it. It's just foolish to trust that as evidence of your salvation. I was a young teen, and my parents were already dead, when I prayed that prayer. I saw how life could end suddenly and needed to be confident of where I was going if I died unexpectedly. I prayed something along the lines of "God, I know I have sinned against You. I believe Jesus died on the cross to pay for my sins. Please enter my life now, and make me the kind of person You want me to be." A counselor then assured me that if I died, I would be going to Heaven.

I still remember the verses used back then by counselors after the altar call.

> *Behold, I stand at the door and knock. If anyone hears my voice and opens the door, I will come in to him and eat with him, and he with me.*
> —Revelation 3:20

> *I write these things to you who believe in the name of the Son of God, that you may know that you have eternal life.*
> —1 John 5:13

I was told that Jesus was knocking on the door to my heart. If I believed in His work on the cross and let Him into my heart, I could be sure that I would go to Heaven one day. I am not denying there is a ton of truth in that statement. Praise God for His finished work on the cross! Those of us who trust in Him really will be saved. This is true. What is also true however is that genuine faith will result in life change. If the transaction was real, the transformation will be also.

My counselor failed to share the context of those verses. As seen earlier, 1 John 5:13 can only be taken in context with the rest of 1 John. The whole book is about signs of a true believer, so in the fifth chapter, John explains that all that was written so "you may know that you have eternal life." How can you know? You'll see in yourself the characteristics mentioned in the first five chapters! Jesus in Revelation 3 is speaking to the person who is "lukewarm." He describes this person as "wretched, pitiable, poor, blind, and naked." He explains that this person will be spit out of His mouth in the end. Jesus is knocking on the door, calling him to repent and truly become saved. Read the passage for yourself. The lukewarm person is not saved! I emphasize this because I can't tell you how many times I've heard people casually or even jokingly talk about how they are lukewarm. I don't get it. Don't you understand that with your acknowledgement, you're admitting you are unsaved—soon to face the wrath of God? No matter how clearly I say it, people still describe themselves as lukewarm with no apparent fear in their voice.

The Fellowship of the Lukewarm

As long as we believe there is such a thing as lukewarm Christians, we will never have unity. I'll say it again: lukewarm people are not Christian! This isn't me saying this. Read Revelation 3. Again, this is *why* Christ is knocking on the door. He's asking you to let Him in because He's not in you yet! You are still in darkness. Light cannot fellowship with darkness (2 Cor. 6:14).

There are still far too many people on the earth who genuinely believe they can be saved by Christ's atoning death without following Him as their Lord. As explained several times in the chapter, these are not saved people. Because so many of them call themselves Christian, it confuses the matter of Christian unity. Whenever you have people who refuse to surrender trying to become perfectly one with those who gladly give their whole lives to Christ, you will have complete chaos. The unsurrendered will always be at odds with the Christ followers, lobbying for their sins to be overlooked and fighting for their own desires in ungodly ways.

Lukewarm people can fellowship just fine with other lukewarm people. They can sit around comforting each other about their sins. They can have Bible studies and support groups and talk about how people can be saved with little or no fruit in their lives. After all, God works differently in different people. They can talk about previous churches that let them down and caused them to sin and run from God. They find common ground in judging the radicals who dare think that Christ calls everyone to deny themselves and pick up crosses. They can exegete passages together, sing together, take communion, and counsel each other. They can even rally together against those who still believe that the commands of Scripture are still valid today.

When Unity Is Easy

In the same way, the unity of the surrendered is almost effortless. Whenever I meet people who resemble a "living sacrifice" (Romans 12:1), having suffered for the gospel, I'm ready to give them the shirt off my back. I feel an immediate affinity and bond in the Spirit. Their lives resemble the life of Christ. Loving them and serving them is an honor because it feels like I am serving Christ Himself. Persecuted believers don't have to work too hard to feel a deep bond with each other.

We've all met people who are so Spirit-filled that they seem to be glowing. Their intimacy with Christ is visible. It conjures thoughts of Moses's glowing face after being with God. When

If you have experienced the
life-changing love of Jesus, you
will be overflowing with love for
God and others. It's that simple.

these overjoyed people encounter one another, they take turns talking about how God has blessed them. God is the hero of all of their stories, and the fellowship is effortless. It's rare to find people overflowing with peace and joy in Christ having conflicts with one another. I've never seen it.

True believers can have unity, and the lukewarm people who insist on calling themselves Christian can have unity. The problems arise when we try to crossbreed. Those who have been persecuted will have an impossible time trying to fellowship with those who believe the gospel should always bring prosperity. Those who love purity can never have peace with those who are constantly saying things like, "I'm sure God doesn't mind if …" Those who put themselves at risk for the gospel will never understand the people who beg them not to. Those experiencing and displaying the love of Christ will always struggle with those who only talk about it.

Why Zacchaeus and the Rich Young Ruler Went to Different Churches

Luke 18 and 19 describe Jesus and His encounters with two rich men. Aside from being filthy rich, they had little in common.

In Luke 18, Jesus encounters a man who was a rich ruler. The man approaches Jesus and asks Him the question that we all wish our friends would ask us: "What must I do to inherit eternal life?" Jesus answered differently than any of us would answer. After reminding him of the commandments, He then says, "One thing you still lack. Sell all that you have and distribute to the poor, and you will have treasure in heaven; and come, follow me." We're told that the rich ruler went away sad, for he was extremely rich. He didn't see the worth of Jesus.

In the following chapter, Jesus surprises Zacchaeus the tax collector (and everyone in Jericho) by inviting Himself to be a guest in Zacchaeus's house. Zacchaeus receives Jesus with joy and, seemingly with no prompting from Jesus, announces that he will be giving half of all his money to the poor and paying back the people he cheated fourfold. Zacchaeus was so beside himself with happiness at the fact that Jesus would enter his home that he *wanted* to sacrifice for Him.

Now, imagine what would happen if these two men were in a fellowship group together. The rich young ruler explains his encounter with Jesus and his frustration that Jesus is not satisfied with the amount he has already sacrificed. Doesn't Jesus appreciate the years he has spent faithfully adhering to the law? The other people begin to comfort him: "Of course Jesus appreciates those things. He didn't literally mean *all* your possessions; that wouldn't be good stewardship." When Zacchaeus tries to interject, sharing some of his experience and why he believes Jesus is worth everything, he is labelled a radical and maybe even considered self-righteous.

Eventually, Zacchaeus becomes discouraged and leaves. In his spirit, he desires oneness with the Body of believers. But there can be no fellowship while he is in the light and they are still stuck in darkness. If they are not following the same Lord, they cannot walk together.

Sanctification versus Surrender

You may be asking, "Isn't the Christian life about a process of sanctification? No one suddenly lives a perfectly holy life at the moment he or she begins following Jesus. Maturity is a process. We can't just walk away from the baby Christians, can we?"

There is a lot of truth in this. Sanctification is indeed a process, but the trouble comes when we begin to equate sanctification with surrender. As a result of sanctification, you will surrender more fully, readily, and joyfully. But it is a mistake to believe that surrender is the mark of maturity and not a requirement for salvation. Hear Jesus' words to those who would follow Him:

> *And he said to all, "If anyone would come after me, let him deny himself and take up his cross daily and follow me. For whoever would save*

his life will lose it, but whoever loses his life for my sake will save it."

                                                    —Luke 9:23–24

As they were going along the road, someone said to him, "I will follow you wherever you go." And Jesus said to him, "Foxes have holes, and birds of the air have nests, but the Son of Man has nowhere to lay his head." To another he said, "Follow me." But he said, "Lord, let me first go and bury my father." And Jesus said to him, "Leave the dead to bury their own dead. But as for you, go and proclaim the kingdom of God." Yet another said, "I will follow you, Lord, but let me first say farewell to those at my home." Jesus said to him, "No one who puts his hand to the plow and looks back is fit for the kingdom of God."

                                                    —Luke 9:57–62

Now great crowds accompanied him, and he turned and said to them, "If anyone comes to me and does not hate his own father and mother and wife and children and brothers and sisters, yes, and even his own life, he cannot be my disciple. Whoever does not bear his own cross and come after me cannot be my disciple. For which of you, desiring to build a tower, does not first sit down and count the cost, whether he has enough to complete it? Otherwise, when he has laid a foundation and is not able to finish, all who see it begin to mock him, saying, 'This man began to build and was not able to finish.' Or what king, going out to encounter another king in war, will not sit down first and deliberate whether he is able with ten thousand to meet him who comes against him with twenty thousand? And if not, while the other is yet a great way off, he sends a delegation and asks for terms of peace. So therefore, any one of you who does not renounce all that he has cannot be my disciple."

—Luke 14:25–33

Jesus did not give any room for a Christian who accepts Him as Savior but is still deciding whether or not He can be Lord. We've created a category of "Christians" that doesn't exist. The true believer must acknowledge Jesus as Lord.

This doesn't mean true believers don't struggle or that they won't be continually laying things at Jesus' feet for the rest of their lives. But deep down, there has to be a desire to become more like Jesus and a willingness to sacrifice out of love for Him. It's about being on a path to perfection. Though no believer on earth has arrived, there are signs of clear progress. If you really are driving from San Francisco to New York, you should consistently find yourself getting closer and closer to your destination.

Some people are in the beginning stages of this journey, and others are moving very slowly. Scripture commands those of us who are strong to patiently bear with these people and build them up in love. When they stumble, we are to restore them in a Spirit of gentleness. If they are truly part of the Body, we have an obligation to nourish and cherish them and to acknowledge our need for them. And this will be frustrating at times. The goal of this section is not by any means to relieve anyone of that responsibility or to promote a spirit of self-righteous zeal.

There is a beautiful, God-honoring unity that can and must take place between weaker and stronger, newer and older believers. This unity must be fought for, and the result will be a wonderful mutual upbuilding. However, I believe there are many people in churches who do not truly follow Jesus, and with them, there can be no unity. It is our responsibility to lovingly confront them and call them higher. But if they remain unchanged, it is *never* our responsibility to lower the bar in the name of unity.

"He who has ears to hear, let him hear" was a phrase that Jesus used often. His point was that not everyone was capable of hearing His message. Only His sheep would be able to hear His voice and come running (John 10:3–5). Even now, as He calls His Bride to become perfectly united, His sheep will hear Him. Many of you reading this have read Acts 4:32–35 and wish the church could act like that again. You want this because He wants this and He dwells in you.

> *Now the full number of those who believed were of one heart and soul, and no one said that any of the things that belonged to him was his own, but they had everything in common. And with great power the apostles were giving their testimony to the resurrection of the Lord Jesus, and great grace was upon them all. There was not a needy person among them, for as many as were owners of lands or houses sold them and brought the proceeds of what was sold and laid it at the apostles' feet, and it was distributed to each as any had need.*
>
> —Acts 4:32–35

Many of us feel envious of the early believers who experienced "the full number" of believers being of "one heart and soul." We dream of living in those days when there was one church filled with people who loved each other deeply and didn't love their things at all. We are the same people whose hearts break when we read church history about the first church split in AD 1054. For over a thousand years, there was only one church. They had their share of problems, but the world only saw one church. After that split, they officially became two factions who excommunicated each other. Some of us hate this and wish it never happened! Years later there were three Christian groups, then four, and each additional split made it more justifiable for the next group to splinter off. Thousands of denominations later, many of us have had enough of this. We are tired of listening to all the different teachers explaining why we have to follow them away from the pack. We want to be one again. The good news is that Jesus wants it even more than we do.

Chapter 3

It's What the World Needs

When I was young, churches would preach about Hell. It was clear to us that the Bible spoke of a severe punishment for sin after we died. This truth gave us a sense of urgency to tell people about Jesus, who came to save them from this destiny. We felt that warning a person about judgment was the most loving thing we could do. This is the way Christians thought for two thousand years.

Then a shift occurred. For the sake of church attendance, pastors began teaching on topics that people wanted to hear about, and Judgment Day didn't make the list. Eventually, pastors who spoke about coming judgment were labeled as fire-and-brimstone preachers trying to frighten people into believing in Jesus. Hell became a taboo subject. People began questioning whether God's wrath could coexist with His grace and love. As our culture began questioning whether it was morally right to punish anyone, Christians began asking a similar question: How could a loving God punish? As it stands today, even the churches who still technically believe in Hell will rarely speak about it. Many have abandoned the doctrine altogether.

This departure from an orthodox view of Hell comforted many Christians because it was more congruent with their lifestyles. Our lack of evangelism didn't make sense if we believed in Hell. If I genuinely believed in a literal Judgment Day with eternal consequences, wouldn't I desperately warn the people I loved? Few people wanted to come across so radical or maniacal. So rather than adjusting our lives, we adjusted our theology. While some try to reinterpret passages about God's wrath, most just ignore them. Everyone is happier this way.

> *Then I saw a great white throne and him who was seated on it. From his presence earth and sky fled away, and no place was found for them. And I saw the dead, great and small, standing before the throne, and books were opened. Then*

another book was opened, which is the book of life. And the dead were judged by what was written in the books, according to what they had done. And the sea gave up the dead who were in it, Death and Hades gave up the dead who were in them, and they were judged, each one of them, according to what they had done. Then Death and Hades were thrown into the lake of fire. This is the second death, the lake of fire. And if anyone's name was not found written in the book of life, he was thrown into the lake of fire.

—Revelation 20:11–15

… since indeed God considers it just to repay with affliction those who afflict you, and to grant relief to you who are afflicted as well as to us, when the Lord Jesus is revealed from heaven with his mighty angels in flaming fire, inflicting vengeance on those who do not know God and on those who do not obey the gospel of our Lord Jesus. They will suffer the punishment of eternal destruction, away from the presence of the Lord and from the glory of his might, when he comes on that day to be glorified in his saints, and to

> *be marveled at among all who have believed,*
> *because our testimony to you was believed.*
>
> —2 Thessalonians 1:6–10

Deceived

If the Scriptures so clearly describe the coming judgment, how can so many who claim to be Christian ignore these passages? The Bible teaches that we have a real Enemy, although recent surveys show that most American Christians don't even believe in the devil anymore.[2] For this chapter's purposes, I'm going to assume that you are one of the ones who do. Wouldn't it make sense that Satan would want us to doubt that judgment was coming? It is the most terrifying or glorious moment in every human's existence, yet we give it little thought. Over these past few decades, he has done a masterful job of distracting us and taking away the fear of judgment. When is the last time you met someone who was passionately warning people about Judgment Day?

> *For we must all appear before the judgment seat*
> *of Christ, so that each one may receive what is*
> *due for what he has done in the body, whether*
> *good or evil. Therefore, knowing the fear of the*
> *Lord, we persuade others. But what we are is*

known to God, and I hope it is known also to
your conscience.

—2 Corinthians 5:10–11

Despite the Enemy's best attempts, there is still a decent-sized remnant of those who, as Paul puts it, know "the fear of the Lord" and "persuade others." Though the numbers may appear to be dwindling, there is still an army of those who are fearfully convinced that they will "appear before the judgment seat of Christ." If you were Satan, how would you discourage them? I know what I would do. I would keep them from the one thing God said would actually save people: unity.

Only let your manner of life be worthy of the
gospel of Christ, so that whether I come and see
you or am absent, I may hear of you that you
are standing firm in one spirit, with one mind
striving side by side for the faith of the gospel, and
not frightened in anything by your opponents.
This is a clear sign to them of their destruction,
but of your salvation, and that from God.

—Philippians 1:27–28

Though most of the world seems to now doubt God's wrath and destruction, the Bible says there is a way to prove His judgment is coming. If Christians would fearlessly share the gospel "in one spirit, with one mind, striving side by side," it would be a "clear sign to them of their destruction." So if I'm the Enemy and my goal is to keep people doubting God's judgment until it's too late, it's obvious what I would do: Divide the church. Take away the power. Eventually, even the committed will become discouraged.

Swearing Paramedics

I was a teenager when I understood what Jesus did on the cross. My natural inclination was to tell my friends about the forgiveness of God and to warn them about the coming judgment. I would cut class to tell people about Jesus. I probably brought a hundred friends to my youth group so they could hear about Jesus. I dreamed of getting the whole school to hear the gospel. I was obsessed with reaching my friends. The longer I was a part of the church, however, the less focused I was on the mission. I spent more and more time with other Christians, and I had fewer and fewer unbelieving friends. We rarely stirred one another to action as God had commanded. Our version of fellowship became going out for coffee and talking about our families.

The more we neglect our mission, the less chance we have of seeing true unity. Our common mission is supposed to lead us toward unity. Lisa and I are united. It's not because we work at it but because we stay focused on our purpose on earth. We stay busy at our common goals of reaching the unreached, caring for the poor, and equipping believers for ministry. The by-product of pursuing a common goal is our oneness. This has been true for twenty-seven years of an insanely happy marriage. Unity is a by-product of mission.

Once we take our eyes off our calling and look at ourselves or each other, conflicts can start creeping in. This has been true of not only us but also of our whole family and church.

Like a marriage that has no purpose, many churches have forgotten the point of their existence. They can quickly focus on the complaints of their people rather than the cries of the lost. We get more emotional over Christians leaving to go to a different church than we do about people dying and going to Hell. Something is horribly wrong when we grieve more deeply over people rejecting us than those who reject their Messiah.

Paul was so fixated on the spread of the gospel that he could rejoice over the gospel being spread, even when it was done with wrong motives.

> Some indeed preach Christ from envy and rivalry, but others from good will. The latter do it out of love, knowing that I am put here for the defense of the gospel. The former proclaim Christ out of selfish ambition, not sincerely but

> *thinking to afflict me in my imprisonment.*
> *What then? Only that in every way, whether*
> *in pretense or in truth, Christ is proclaimed,*
> *and in that I rejoice.*
>
> —Philippians 1:15–18

He understood the urgency of the situation. It wasn't hard for him to put his feelings aside when he saw that the true gospel was being preached. People were purposely attacking him, and it didn't faze him—as long as the gospel was proclaimed. It's like a paramedic swearing at you while he's trying to save your wife's life. You can overlook your own feelings when someone you love is in serious danger. There is no danger greater than an eternity apart from God. We need God to revive our concern for the destiny of unbelievers. It's when we care about them enough that we will put aside our differences to reach them together.

I Have a Better Idea

Sometimes the dream of a united church feels unattainable, so we busy ourselves with goals that are within reach. While we may believe that our oneness would impact the world, we are nowhere close to that, so we find other methods of attracting the lost. God's method seems too hard, so we come up with "better" ideas. We need to be so careful with this reasoning. It seems dangerously close to what Saul did, and it cost him the kingdom.

In 1 Samuel 13, Samuel tells Saul that God is going to tear the kingdom away from him and give it to someone else—a man after His own heart. Just two chapters before, we're told how the Spirit of God rushed upon Saul and how he mustered all the people of Israel to accomplish a great victory over their enemies. We see in chapters 10 and 11 that when Saul is criticized by others, he holds his peace and chooses not to take revenge when given the opportunity. Saul glorifies God for the military victory, sacrificing peace offerings and rejoicing before Him. He seems like an effective leader and a wise man. So what went wrong?

In chapter 13, Saul is about to go to war with the Philistines. Samuel had told Saul that he would come in seven days to offer sacrifices and entreat the favor of the Lord before the army went to battle. So Saul waits seven days, but Samuel does not come. The people grow tired of waiting and Saul does not want to go to war without sacrificing to God, so he offers the sacrifice himself. Doesn't that make sense to you? It does to me. Samuel was late, Saul needed to go to war, but he knew he shouldn't go without making an offering first. Were I in his position, I could see myself doing the same thing. It feels like a very logical decision.

God doesn't see it that way. He sends Samuel to rebuke Saul for his foolishness and tells him that because of his disobedience, his kingdom will not continue. It seems like a harsh punishment for an understandable offense.

In chapter 15, we see a very similar scenario play out. Saul is commanded to go strike down the Amalekites and destroy everything, even down to their livestock. But Saul and the people, seeing that some of the animals are very good, keep back the best portion of them to offer as a sacrifice to the Lord. Again, I feel like this is a reasonable decision. The animals are going to die regardless, and the people aren't taking the livestock for themselves out of greed, so they just want to sacrifice them to God. But when Samuel hears of it, he responds:

> *Has the LORD as great delight in*
> *burnt offerings and sacrifices,*
> *as in obeying the voice of the LORD?*
> *Behold, to obey is better than sacrifice,*
> *and to listen than the fat of rams.*
> *For rebellion is as the sin of divination,*
> *and presumption is as iniquity and idolatry.*
> *Because you have rejected the*
> *word of the LORD,*
> *he has also rejected you*
> *from being king.*
> —1 Samuel 15:22–23

My fear is that,

perhaps without even

realizing it, we've fallen into

the very dangerous habit of

neglecting God's commands

in favor of our logic.

In the words of John Snyder, "Innovation, tradition, sincerity, sacrifice, good intentions—not one or all can substitute for obedience to God regarding how He desires to be worshipped."[3] On the outside, Saul's errors do not look that serious. But underlying them is a very serious heart condition: Saul does not treat God's words with the appropriate reverence and awe. Because of this, he thinks it appropriate to *add* to God's instructions some of his own reasoning. The lesson of this story is that no matter how good or logical it seems, it is *never* appropriate to modify God's commands in light of human reasoning. At the root of that kind of behavior is pride, thinking that somehow in our wisdom we have considered something God neglected to notice. God treats this presumption as idolatry.

This prideful, idolatrous spirit is running rampant in the church today, disguised like Saul's with good intentions and pragmatism. God made it clear that striving together in unity would work, but we reason our way into new methods.

I don't pretend to understand exactly why unity would cause unbelievers to suddenly believe in their coming judgment and our salvation. But my responsibility is not to understand why; my responsibility is to be obedient. Saul may not have understood why it was important for all the livestock of the Amalekites to be destroyed, but it should have been enough for Him that God had commanded it. That is what it means to accept Jesus as *Lord* and *King*.

Betting on a Sure Thing

We live in a time when innovation is practically worshipped. We're always looking for ways to make things more efficient, more effective, more appealing. Seeing the success that this sort of thinking wrought in the secular world, people in the church began—with good intentions I believe—to apply the same tactics to ministry to see if this approach would yield similar "success." We've come up with hundreds of innovative ideas for how to get people into churches: concerts, plays, programs, sports, shorter services, better childcare, you name it.

My fear is that, perhaps without even realizing it, we've fallen into the very dangerous habit of neglecting God's commands in favor of our logic. For example, if I invite the most famous Christian artist to do a concert at my church, I'm sure to get a crowd of people, maybe even some open-minded unbelievers. I can give a gospel presentation in the middle and an altar call at the end, and through a couple hours of work, I'm almost guaranteed to have some kind of positive response. On the other hand, if I commit to becoming like family with a few other believers, I could spend years pouring time and energy into building those relationships, and I have no idea how that is going to affect any unbelievers. I would have to put all my hope in a promise.

When I look at those two options, there's no question which one makes more sense in the flesh. Many people stop right there and make their decision. But I would ask you to consider:

- Does marching around a city seven times and blowing trumpets sound like the most effective way to conquer a city?
- Does a little shepherd boy with a slingshot sound like the best candidate to defeat a giant warrior?

This list could be expanded at length, but you get the point. God often asks people to pursue strategies that don't make the most logical sense. If they did make sense to us, we wouldn't need faith. And without faith, it is impossible to please God (Hebrews 11:6)

God's ways are not our ways. He has not asked us to strategize; He has asked us to obey. It seems simple, so why haven't we obeyed? I can't speak for you, but I know what usually keeps me from staying committed to His plan: disbelief.

Unbelievable

A lot of truths are expressed in this short passage of Scripture that are impossible to believe apart from a miracle. I'm going to ask you to read this slowly. Ask yourself if you really believe this is possible.

> *I do not ask for these only, but also for those*
> *who will believe in me through their word,*
> *that they may all be one, just as you, Father,*
> *are in me, and I in you, that they also may be*
> *in us, so that the world may believe that you*
> *have sent me. The glory that you have given*
> *me I have given to them, that they may be one*
> *even as we are one, I in them and you in me,*
> *that they may become perfectly one, so that the*
> *world may know that you sent me and loved*
> *them even as you loved me.*
>
> —John 17:20–23

I want to look at several phrases in this prayer, but first I want to remind you of the Person praying this prayer. Don't forget that in Jesus "all the fullness of God was pleased to dwell" (Col. 1:19). His cry for unity is the very cry of God Himself. While I have always been intrigued by His prayer, I have not always taken it seriously and literally.

"That they may all be one"

Jesus prays that "all" believers would be "one." Be honest, do you anticipate this happening in your lifetime? Sometimes I consider the possibility of us all taking baby steps in this direction. I usually lack the faith to believe that all believers could jump fully on board. I know too many people who are extremely critical and divisive, and they have been this way for years. Therein lies my problem: I keep looking at people. This isn't about talking people into unity. It's about praying like Jesus prayed. My disbelief came from spending too much time thinking about how to convince people and not enough time praying in faith. Are we saying there is something too difficult for God to do? Let's pray in faith as Jesus prayed, "that they may all be one." Let's trust that our prayers can change us all.

"Just as you, Father, are in me, and I in you"

Just as? Earlier, we looked at the sacred mystery of the triune God. A perfect union from all of eternity past. Jesus is not just asking that we simply get along. He is not just saying that we need to feel some form of love toward each other. He is praying for a union that resembles what He has with the Father. When is the last time you saw that as a possibility with anyone in the church, let alone everyone?

"That they also may be in us"

If reading this does nothing to you, something is wrong with your heart. Jesus is showing His desire to be one with us. He is asking that we, as His united followers, would be connected into the Trinity in some sense! I honestly can't get my mind around this, but when Jesus prays that we be united so that we can "be in" the Father and Son, how can we ever downplay unity? For those of us who have faced a lifetime of rejections, it takes tremendous faith to believe that Christ petitions for this union. There is something so much more powerful available to us than anything we've experienced if we will lean into what Jesus is praying here.

"The glory that you have given me I have given to them"

This is what makes our unity with Him and with each other possible. He has given us glory. I come from a tradition that tends to focus on our depravity. That's not a bad thing. It keeps us from believing there was anything good in ourselves that warranted God's favor. The problem is that we focused so much on our depravity that we didn't praise Him enough for our glory! Christ made us beautiful. Because of the cross, we are holy and blameless children of God. The resurrected Christ has given us His glory. If we only stare at our own sin and the sin of others, we will be blinded to the glory we possess.

"That they may become perfectly one"

Perfection? This is the point when everyone points out that this can't happen until we get to Heaven. If that's true, however, then Jesus wouldn't finish the sentence "so that the world may know that you sent me and loved them even as you loved me." He's talking about here and now so the whole world can see it! Our perfect oneness is proof that Jesus is sent by the Father and that the Father loves us "even as" He loves Jesus.

How are we supposed to believe all this? It all sounds too far-fetched. We are supposed to believe that all believers could be given His glory to become perfectly one, just like the Father and Son. The world will observe our perfect union with God and each other and become convinced that Jesus is the Messiah and that we are loved immensely by the Father! It all just sounds too good to be true. The promise sounds too glorious, and the obstacles look too massive. But what choice do we have other than to fight for this? Wander around in the wilderness a few more years?

We need to see this as our promised land. Because we live on the other side of the cross, it is far easier to believe. It seems outrageous that a church so divided could become perfectly one, but nothing is more outrageous than the cross. Remember, we believe in a God who sent His Son to die on a cross to draw us near to Him. Why is it hard to believe that He would find a way to draw us all together? This was His prayer. This isn't one of those things *we* want, hoping that it aligns with His will. We worship a God who gets what *He* wants. He wanted us, and He made a way to get us. He wants our unity to impact the world, so I believe He will find a way to bring us together.

We need to keep our eyes on
the mission and realize that
we need each other if we're
going to pull this off.

The Stakes Are High

Do you understand how significant this is? It's not a matter of getting along with a sibling you can't stand because your mom said to. This is a matter of *the world believing in Jesus!* The stakes are that high. And this is Jesus' plan for showing the world who He truly is! If I tell you to find some superficial form of unity so we look less embarrassing as Christians, you might be excused for lacking sufficient motivation. But now that you can clearly see in Jesus' prayer that deep unity among His followers is Jesus' plan for bringing the world to see Him, I hope your motivation is through the roof!

Perhaps it will help if you stop thinking about crowds coming to Jesus. Put a face to it. Maybe it's your dad, your sister, cousin, best friend, or coworker who isn't interested in following Jesus. Imagine they encounter a church so united that they realize Jesus is who He claimed to be. They don't just hear someone preaching about the grace, mercy, and sacrifice of Christ, but they see believers model this love with each other. This opens their eyes. Now is the sacrifice worth it?

Nothing else we could attempt as a means for reaching the lost comes with this promised empowerment. We're free to choose our own methods, but honestly, I'm embarrassed that I ever thought my strategies would be better than Jesus'.

Perhaps this sense of purpose is what has been missing in our failed attempts at unity. As I said at the beginning of this chapter, when Lisa and I are fighting side by side for the mission Jesus gave us, it keeps us from fighting *with* each other in our marriage. A common mission brings oneness.

Too often, we do the very thing Paul warned us not to do in 1 Corinthians 12:14–26. We look at another member of the Body of Christ and say, "I have no need of you." That's what our disunity amounts to. Obviously our doctrinal convictions matter. I'm not trying to talk anyone out of their firm beliefs regarding the teaching of Scripture. But Paul's point here aligns so closely with Jesus' prayer in John 17. He's saying that we need every member of the Body if we are going to function the way God designed us to. Disunity isn't just ugly; it makes us dysfunctional. We cannot be the presence and force in this world that God intended if we're actively jettisoning essential parts of our Body.

Instead, we need to keep our eyes on the mission and realize that we need each other if we're going to pull this off. Above all, we need the empowerment of God's Spirit, but that is exactly Paul's point in 1 Corinthians 12: the Spirit has empowered us *by spreading His gifts among the whole church family!* So when we compromise on unity, we're cutting ourselves off from the power of the Spirit and thereby undermining our mission.

No Plan B

Choosing God's method will not guarantee you a big following—in fact, it will probably cause people to leave. But I don't want to make the mistake Saul did and under peer pressure begin to panic and switch to another method. If Saul had waited a few more hours, he might have lost a few followers but he could have kept the favor of the Lord.

Jesus has said that when we become perfectly one, the world will believe that Jesus was sent by God and that God loves the world *even as* He loves His Son. And so, no matter how hard or illogical or uncomfortable it gets, I can't quit pursuing this. I'm not necessarily saying we shouldn't do any other forms of outreach, but they need to be accompanied by an equal if not greater effort to encourage the church toward this oneness that Scripture promises will reach the lost. The gospel message is incomplete without the picture of the unified church. There is no plan B.

Chapter 4

It Starts with Repentance

Are you the problem?

I have to admit that when I began writing this book, I hoped to confront the people who were dividing the church. It didn't take long for God to show me all the ways I have added to the problem. Initially, I thought it was just something I struggled with in the past. But the more I studied the Scriptures, the more I saw that I still had plenty of work to do. My point: don't assume divisions were caused by someone else. Revivals begin with repentance, and we can all benefit from asking God to reveal our shortsightedness.

Search me, O God, and know my heart!
Try me and know my thoughts!
And see if there be any grievous way in me,
and lead me in the way everlasting!
—Psalm 139:23–24

You're Not as Dumb as I Thought You Were

I first fell in love with Jesus in a Baptist church. The youth pastor was clear in articulating the work of the cross, and some of the people were eager to love me as family. One couple even took me into their home when I had nowhere else to live. Those were wonderful and life-changing days. I thank God for that church, and I am still in contact with some of those who began loving me forty years ago. (A quick shout out to Stan, Ken, Mike, Vicky, Debbie, Cindy, Todd, and Dawn!)

Because I found so much life through that church, I accepted all their theology. I questioned nothing. Why would I? It was here that I found Jesus, truth, life, and love. To question any of their doctrine would have felt a bit disloyal toward the people to whom I owe so much.

I later attended Bible college and seminary to learn how to study and teach the Bible. Again, I felt so much gratitude for the school that gave me tools to study the Scriptures. A couple of professors in particular not only taught me but seemed to genuinely care about me. Out of loyalty once again, I held to all the doctrine I was taught.

Years after seminary, I began meeting more and more Christians who held to different doctrines from what I was taught. As a staunch cessationist, I literally got knots in my stomach whenever I met someone who claimed to be Christian yet spoke in tongues or claimed to have a supernatural gift of prophecy. I viewed them as ignorant and dangerous.

Then I got to know some of them.

One of the first was a pastor named Jack Hayford. I had agreed to join a board for a ministry that cared for the inner-city poor. Jack happened to be on this board as well. I held a lot of assumptions about Jack because his name often came up in my school. I also held a belief that those who believed in these supernatural gifts did so because they were too lazy to study the Scriptures, that they relied on visions from God rather than careful study and obedience to biblical commands. As I got to know Jack, I saw a man who loved Jesus deeply and was faithful to studying the Bible. When I first heard him teach, I assumed it was going to be shallow—not nearly to the level of scholarship of this recent seminary grad. I was shocked as he explained an Old Testament text, giving historical context and dissecting the Hebrew in a way of which I was incapable. He shattered my paradigm.

Over the years, I was able to observe Jack's character and saw an overflow of love, joy, peace, patience, and other fruit of the Spirit. Since then I have met many charismatics who don't study the Word and are complacent toward sin. However, I have also met many who are the opposite. As they have patiently explained their interpretations of Scripture, I saw that their conclusions weren't as ridiculous as I once thought. Before this, I had only learned their theology from the biased perspective of those who staunchly disagreed. I had never actually spoken to them or read their books. After doing so, I not only better understood their reasoning but I came to agree with them in some of their teachings. For example, the apostle Paul says in 1 Corinthians 14:39, "So, my brothers, earnestly desire to prophesy, and do not forbid speaking in tongues." I now understand why charismatics interpret this to mean that we should desire prophecy and not forbid tongues.

Especially over the past two decades, I have rubbed shoulders with leaders of many different denominations. I questioned some of them on their theology. Even after they answered me, I still disagreed with some of their conclusions but I saw that they had studied diligently. Sometimes I would begin these conversations being 99 percent sure that I was right, and I would leave being about 70 percent sure that I was right. Other times, I concluded that I was wrong (which I always hate!). I don't feel wishy-washy on my convictions, but I am learning that it's possible and sometimes healthy to reexamine my understanding of Scripture—even when that means learning from someone I don't agree with on everything.

As an example, I am currently 90 percent sure that I have been wrong about my belief that Christ is not present in the Eucharist. I'm probably about 70 percent sure that the denominations that hold the most accurate view of the Eucharist are those that marvel at the real but mysterious presence of Christ. I'm about 65 percent sure that transubstantiation as most understand it is inaccurate. I am about 95 percent sure that I was wrong about my cessationist view of the gifts.

When I say things like this, I realize that some readers want to fight me on these things. I understand. I was there. I once thought all charismatics were shallow and dangerous heretics. I once thought all Catholics were unsaved and lifeless idol worshipers. I never dreamed that I would actually have friends who were charismatic Catholics and that I would love them as brothers. I still have serious doctrinal disagreements with many charismatics and all Catholics, but with those I have had the opportunity to befriend, we share love and unity that goes deeper than I would have imagined.

Fast forward forty years, and I still hold to the basic foundational truths I was taught in my early years. I still spend time alone reading the Scriptures daily. I still believe that salvation is by grace alone through faith in Christ. I really haven't deviated much from my Baptist roots, but I have come to the realization that there are topics I never truly researched for myself. I just assumed what I was taught without ever taking the time to learn from those on "the other side."

I share all that background to show that I have been on a quest to find truth about all sorts of issues over the years. That journey continues. Some would criticize me in saying that I shouldn't preach about something unless I am sure of it. My question is: How sure do I have to be? 100 percent? 90 percent? 51 percent? When I was younger, I was 100 percent convinced of certain doctrines that I now highly doubt. The older I get, the less inclined I am to be 100 percent sure of anything. One of the few things I am sure of is that I only "know in part" (1 Cor. 13:12), so I try to carry myself with the appropriate humility.

A Call to Humility

Many Christian leaders today view themselves as defenders of truth. They're the ones holding the line against the tide of heretical charismatics, the arrogant Reformed camp, or whomever your camp views as the "enemy." Many of us have so much loyalty to our circles that we have never stopped to ask: Are we really even seeking truth anymore, or are we just defending what we already believe? When we hear some sort of divergent truth or something that doesn't quite sit right given our theological foundation, where do we run for an explanation? We run to our own people, the ones we trust for natural reasons (they were the ones who led us to the Lord, the people our family trusts, whatever it is). And this makes sense. *But*, it does mean that we really only ever hear one side of an argument.

It's worth asking the question: Why are you so sure that your camp's theology is better than mine? It comes back to epistemology: how truth is acquired. If you are reading this book, you probably agree with me that Scripture is the basis for truth. If we all agree on that, then why do we have so many theological differences? Because there are differences in interpretation. How, then, do you determine who has the best interpretation of Scripture? Is it whoever is most intelligent? Whoever has the best reasoning? The most humble and loving person? The one who is most in tune with the Holy Spirit? Again, we will find ourselves at an impasse because even if we did know which of those measures should be used to determine whom to listen to, there are no objective ways to measure those qualities.

If we believe 1 Corinthians 2, it seems unlikely that arrogant people would have the firmest grasp of truth. After confronting division and arrogance in chapter 1, Paul explains in chapter 2 that spiritual truths can only be taught by the Holy Spirit Himself. In this fascinating passage, he explains that a natural person cannot understand spiritual truth no matter how brilliant he or she may be.

I point this out not to discourage anyone from studying hard to find truth but to caution you against arrogance. You may consciously or subconsciously believe that you've got everything right and that the beliefs of other people or denominations must be completely unfounded, to the point where you will not even engage in an open conversation with someone of a different view. This kind of pride is only going to hinder you from hearing the Spirit of truth. If God gives grace to the humble, it's hard to imagine that those who are most arrogant would be the most accurate.

Paul talks about this in 1 Corinthians 13, a chapter which many of us know at least part of by heart. At the end of his famous description of love, he writes in verses 8–12:

> *Love never ends. As for prophecies, they will pass away; as for tongues, they will cease; as for knowledge, it will pass away. For we know in part and we prophesy in part, but when the perfect comes, the partial will pass away. When I was a child, I spoke like a child, I thought like a child, I reasoned like a child. When I became a man, I gave up childish ways. For now we see*

in a mirror dimly, but then face to face. Now I
know in part; then I shall know fully, even as I
have been fully known.

Any knowledge of God that we think we have here on Earth, everything that the most brilliant scholars have ever grasped of heavenly truth, is like a dim reflection of real truth in a mirror. Not like one of the mirrors we have today, but like a piece of shiny metal that you can just barely make out your face in. It's childish. It's temporary. If you're having a hard time accepting that or are starting to feel defensive, stop right now and check your heart. Do you really think you have God figured out? Do you really think you have 100 percent correct theology? If so, that's a scary place to be.

About a year ago, I was speaking to a friend who is a special needs teacher. He has a heart to reach his students with the gospel. He shared that, for a while, he wrestled with wondering how the gospel could be communicated to and accepted by kids who are nonverbal. But then God opened his eyes to see the foolishness of that kind of thinking. Did he think God didn't have to stoop down too far to accommodate his own intelligence level? How could we possibly think that God can't accommodate people without some of the capabilities we have, as though we're somehow on a "closer level" to God? As though God could make the jump down to

All of us have an incomplete, flawed knowledge of God. Without humility, we will never have unity.

my level of intelligence but others are too much of a stretch? How disgustingly arrogant that is! I was so convicted by this truth. Somehow, in my imagination, I had been thinking of God communicating with the heavenly beings in English at my level of comprehension. The truth is that God probably communicates in a mode that I can barely fathom.

I have said many times that I believe one of the most important passages for this generation is Isaiah 55:8–9 where God says "For my thoughts are not your thoughts, neither are your ways my ways, declares the LORD. For as the heavens are higher than the earth, so are my ways higher than your ways and my thoughts than your thoughts." In many ways, we have lost a sense of the true holiness of God, and that has caused pride to grow and fester in the church. Everyone seems to start out with the assumption that his or her opinion of God is right, rather than recognizing that *all* of us have an incomplete, flawed knowledge of God. Without humility, we will never have unity. More importantly, without humility, we cannot be in a right relationship with God.

Defenders of Unity

Imagine what it could be like if, rather than viewing themselves as the defenders of truth, Christian leaders lived like it was their God-given duty to defend the unity of the Church. I see this spirit in the early church fathers, and there's

something so beautiful and attractive about it. When disagreements arose and heretical beliefs began to threaten the
Church, they called ecumenical councils to gather individuals from *both* sides. They confronted each other face to face
with the goal of discerning truth, reaching consensus, pro-
moting peace, and protecting a unified Church. From these
councils we get statements like the Nicene Creed, developed
in the First Council of Nicaea. Listen to the words here:

> We believe in one God, the Father, the
> Almighty, maker of heaven and earth, of all
> that is, seen and unseen.
>
> We believe in one Lord, Jesus Christ, the
> only Son of God, eternally begotten of the
> Father, God from God, Light from Light,
> true God from true God, begotten, not
> made, of one Being with the Father. Through
> him all things were made.
>
> For us and for our salvation he came
> down from heaven: by the power of the Holy
> Spirit he became incarnate from the Virgin
> Mary, and was made man.
>
> For our sake he was crucified under
> Pontius Pilate; he suffered death and was
> buried. On the third day he rose again in
> accordance with the Scriptures; he ascended

into heaven and is seated at the right hand of the Father. He will come again in glory to judge the living and the dead, and his kingdom will have no end.

We believe in the Holy Spirit, the Lord, the giver of life, who proceeds from the Father and the Son. With the Father and the Son he is worshiped and glorified. He has spoken through the Prophets. We believe in one holy catholic and apostolic Church. We acknowledge one baptism for the forgiveness of sins. We look for the resurrection of the dead, and the life of the world to come. Amen.

Imagine the early church fathers coming together, not ignoring or hiding their differences but acknowledging them and working through them. Imagine those early leaders together pooling their wisdom and writing a creed with the earnest hope and prayer that it would serve as the theological anchor and foundation for a strong, unified Church in their day and the days to come. Doesn't that sound infinitely more attractive than what you see today—thousands of leaders squabbling with each other and trying to convince you to join their camp?

Rather than fighting for followers or individual glory, the early church prioritized the glory of God and His unified Bride. Instead of searching for reasons to denounce people, they sought common ground to bring Christians together. We need to start asking ourselves hard, honest questions. Can we speak with as much confidence about the purity of our motives?

God's Zeal for His Temple

I have never been more afraid of causing division. After restudying 1 Corinthians 3 in context of the first three chapters, God showed me that I have not been serious enough about my own divisive speech and actions. As a result, I have recently spent some time confessing things I have said and done, consciously or subconsciously, that have aided rather than prevented the splintering of His Church.

Paul doesn't spend just the first chapter of 1 Corinthians speaking of boasting and division. This theme runs throughout his letter. In chapter 6, he confronts the fact that believers were suing each other, for the world to see, instead of taking on a Christlike attitude of "why not rather suffer wrong?" In chapter 7, he addresses their divorces. In chapter 8, he confronts their arrogance that is destroying their brothers. In chapter 11, he says their celebration of the Lord's Supper does more harm than good because of their divisions. In chapter 12, he reminds them they are a Body and therefore it's ridiculous for one part to look at any other part with an "I have no need of you" attitude. Chapters 13–14 explain that it's their lack of love that causes even their spiritual gifts to be used for boasting and dividing rather than building each other up.

From start to finish, Paul's first letter to the Corinthians was meant to bring them together in love and lead them to repent of their divisions. For me, nothing is as terrifying as God's warning in chapter 3.

In the first four verses, Paul explicitly states that they are immature babies and that this is shown by their divisions. The fact that there exists "strife" and boasting in people proves they are unspiritual. In verses 5–9, he reminds them that he and Apollos are nothing, just servants doing their duty. His point is that the Corinthian believers need to stop talking about them. In verses 10–15, he tells them that Judgment Day is coming and that's the only time we will know the real truth. It's an encouragement to stop judging the works of others and worry about yourself. That leads up to the most terrifying warning, in my opinion:

> *Do you not know that you are God's temple and that God's Spirit dwells in you? If anyone destroys God's temple, God will destroy him. For God's temple is holy, and you are that temple.*
>
> —1 Corinthians 3:16–17

If any of you can read a phrase like "God will destroy him" without any degree of trembling, that's scary. Don't lose the weight of a statement like that. God's zeal toward His holy temple is ferocious, and that's a good thing. All our careless words that lead to the damaging of brothers and sisters will be judged. All our boasting in any leader apart from Christ is sparking these divisions which destroy the temple, "so let no one boast in men" (v. 21).

God have mercy on us!

At this point, we should all have a holy moment. All the opinions of those inside and outside our camps should mean nothing in light of our impending judgment by a Holy God. This was Paul's attitude in the following verses:

> *But with me it is a very small thing that I should be judged by you or by any human court. In fact, I do not even judge myself. For I am not aware of anything against myself, but I am not thereby acquitted. It is the Lord who judges me. Therefore do not pronounce judgment before the time, before the Lord comes, who will bring to light the things now hidden in darkness and will disclose the purposes of the heart. Then each one will receive his commendation from God.*
>
> —1 Corinthians 4:3–5

Too often we fixate

on our disagreements,

and we feel like we can't

worship with such big elephants

in the room. We don't see that

God is infinitely larger than

our elephants.

If these verses don't move you to humbly examine your actions before your Creator and Judge, you have serious issues. We can't allow ourselves to be preoccupied with what people think. I get it: making changes toward embracing brothers and sisters outside of your circle will be met with opposition. But are you going to allow that to supersede your fear of God?

> For am I now seeking the approval of man, or of God? Or am I trying to please man? If I were still trying to please man, I would not be a servant of Christ.
>
> —Galatians 1:10

Good Bragging

> I appeal to you, brothers, by the name of our Lord Jesus Christ, that all of you agree, and that there be no divisions among you, but that you be united in the same mind and the same judgment. For it has been reported to me by Chloe's people that there is quarreling among you, my brothers. What I mean is that each one of you says, "I follow Paul," or "I follow Apollos," or "I follow Cephas," or "I follow Christ." Is Christ

divided? Was Paul crucified for you? Or were
you baptized in the name of Paul?
                                   —1 Corinthians 1:10–13

Divisions were sown in the Corinthian church as individuals began comparing leaders and picking which leader to rally behind. Separate groups formed who quarreled with each other about which leader was best. The advantage they had on us was that their leaders weren't enjoying the praise. Rather than fueling the "Paul fans," Paul begs them to stop. He tells them that we are all fools who believe in a simple message that is to be preached simply. He reminds them of where they came from and that they had nothing to boast about. In fact, God chose fools "***so that*** *no human being might boast in the presence of God*" (1 Cor. 1:29). They were a bunch of foolish sinners saved by Jesus, so boasting in Jesus is the only boasting that makes sense.

Let the one who boasts, boast in the Lord.
                                   —1 Corinthians 1:31

When godly people get together, they boast about Jesus. They can't help but tell stories about their experiences with Him and the joy they find in Him. God is honored, and they themselves leave those times even more amazed by Christ.

When we hear stories of how Christ works in others, it makes us want to praise Him even more. It's a sanctified snowball effect. There should be no end to the things in Christ that we can boast about.

When "Christians" gather today, they boast about their favorite teacher and how well he or she explains the Word. They talk about churches, worship bands, schools, theologians, books, songs, denominations, ministries, political issues, social issues, pastors, singers, and so on. Inevitably disagreements arise about who is most accurate, anointed, intelligent, or wise. Once you pick your favorite leader, you head to the island where everyone worships him or her. Suddenly you feel unity again because you surround yourself with people who agree with you regarding your leader or your theology. You agree on the strengths of your leader, and you agree on the weaknesses of the other camps.

As long as you stay on your island, there's harmony. At least until someone on the island comes up with a new idea and rallies his or her own crew to head to another island.

Seriously consider what would happen if we could have a reset and start over. This time around, all of us who called ourselves Christian promised to boast in no one except Jesus. Every time we got together we would spend time boasting about Him, sharing stories of His goodness toward us. This doesn't mean disagreements wouldn't still come up, but they wouldn't be the centerpiece. We wouldn't be bragging about ourselves, our possessions, our knowledge, our achievements—or anyone else's. We would spend our days boasting of the infinite grace of God and listening to others do the same. Hopefully, that sounds like paradise to you. Now imagine your group was merged with another group that was living in exactly the same way. Would it be hard to live together with another group of people like that? Maybe unity really is that simple.

Too often we fixate on our disagreements, and we feel like we can't worship with such big elephants in the room. We don't see that God is infinitely larger than our elephants, so He is worthy of our attention and praise even if we sit amid a herd of elephants.

If that new island sounds like Paradise, it's because it is. The unity of Heaven is found in their unified boasting: *"Thy will be done on earth as it is in Heaven."*[4]

Chapter 5

It Comes with Maturity

Ephesians 4 is clear: everyone in ministry should have a common goal. Our job is to help all members of the Body of Christ mature.

> *And he gave the apostles, the prophets, the evangelists, the shepherds and teachers, to equip the saints for the work of ministry, for building up the body of Christ, until we all attain to the unity of the faith and of the knowledge of the Son of God, to mature manhood, to the measure of the stature of the fullness of Christ,*

*so that we may no longer be children, tossed
to and fro by the waves and carried about by
every wind of doctrine, by human cunning, by
craftiness in deceitful schemes. Rather, speaking
the truth in love, we are to grow up in every
way into him who is the head, into Christ, from
whom the whole body, joined and held together
by every joint with which it is equipped, when
each part is working properly, makes the body
grow so that it builds itself up in love.*

—Ephesians 4:11–16

God has gifted His Church with apostles, prophets, evangelists, shepherds, and teachers. Their job is to "equip the saints for the work of ministry," and they are supposed to do this "until we all attain to the unity of the faith." If leaders are doing their jobs properly, the outcome should be mature saints who are out doing ministry while becoming more united. The Bible describes a type of training that results in equipped and unified workers.

The Fatal Detour on the Path to Maturity

As Christian leaders, most of us know that our job is to bring people to maturity:

Him we proclaim, warning everyone and teaching everyone with all wisdom, that we may present everyone mature in Christ. For this I toil, struggling with all his energy that he powerfully works within me.

—Colossians 1:28–29

God's desire is that His children become "perfect and complete, lacking in nothing" (James 1:4). The New Testament is filled with passages describing how a mature person lives and acts:

For this very reason, make every effort to supplement your faith with virtue, and virtue with knowledge, and knowledge with self-control, and self-control with steadfastness, and steadfastness with godliness, and godliness with brotherly affection, and brotherly affection with love.

—2 Peter 1:5–7

But the fruit of the Spirit is love, joy, peace, patience, kindness, goodness, faithfulness, gentleness, self-control; against such things there is no law.

—Galatians 5:22–23

Put on then, as God's chosen ones, holy and beloved, compassionate hearts, kindness, humility, meekness, and patience, bearing with one another and, if one has a complaint against another, forgiving each other; as the Lord has forgiven you, so you also must forgive. And above all these put on love, which binds everything together in perfect harmony.

—Colossians 3:12–14

The simplest way to understand how a mature believer should look is to study the life of Christ. Obviously, there's no better picture of a mature Christian than Christ. In Him we see love, mercy, compassion, boldness, holiness, forgiveness, and sacrifice personified. He was the epitome of every fruit of the Spirit. The way He handled the Scriptures and the way He handled people is the standard for anyone who calls himself or herself Christian.

How do you train someone to become like Jesus, though? Are love and joy and peace things we can actually teach in a classroom? Jesus modeled these characteristics while He walked alongside His disciples. They experienced hardship and suffering together. They experienced the power of the Spirit together. They learned love by watching Him love. True discipleship involves living life together, caring for the lost and hurting together, and experiencing victories and disappointments together.

In America, when we want to train leaders, we send them to classes and schools. By using classrooms as the primary venue for training, we end up focusing on the one thing we can teach in a classroom: information.

While knowledge is a big part of maturing as a believer, many have made it the only part. This has wreaked havoc on the church and actually prevents real maturity from happening. Look at the following diagram, and then I'll explain it.

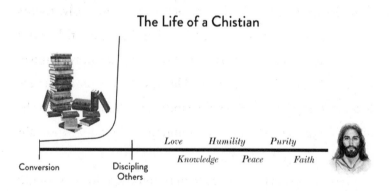

The Life of a Chistian

Love   Humility   Purity
Knowledge   Peace   Faith

Conversion   Discipling
                    Others

The road to maturity (Christlikeness) involves continual growth in intimacy with God, humility, holiness, faith, hope, power, love, joy, peace, and so on. Along the path to maturity we lead others, baptizing them and teaching them to obey all that God commanded. But many never reach maturity

This is what God
wants: groups of mature
believers who show the world
supernatural love for each other.
The love component of church
is not negotiable.

because they never lead others. Instead of becoming teachers, they stay in a constant state of learning (Hebrews 5:12). Some refuse to lead, while others spend a lifetime believing they aren't ready. To prepare themselves, they start taking classes. They read Christian books (like this one!). They dig into sermon after sermon, believing this is what it means to grow in maturity. But this is where the great deception begins.

Rather than staying on the path to maturity (which includes increasing in knowledge), they take a different road that focuses primarily on attaining information. While they are increasing in knowledge, they are not growing in humility. While they are filling their minds with information, they are not emptying themselves for the needy. They aren't leading others by living life with them and modeling the fruit of the Spirit. As a result, we have people who see themselves as mature because they know so many things about Scripture but their lives look nothing like that of Christ. They don't take steps of faith, risking their lives and livelihoods for the sake of the gospel.

The chart shows that you can actually be a further distance from maturity if you continue up the road of information without growing in love. Paul describes this when he says that "'knowledge' puffs up, but love builds up" (1 Cor. 8:1). Acquiring knowledge without using it in love for others leads to a pride that takes you further from Christ. It leads to a blocking of God's grace and a welcoming of His opposition: "God opposes the proud but gives grace to the humble" (James 4:6). In our current mode of church life, we wouldn't dare call anyone immature who has a wealth of biblical knowledge. However, I would argue that there are many baby scholars out there. They have gone far on the chart, but they are headed the wrong direction.

Warning Signs

One of the most visible signs that a person is heading in the wrong direction is a lack of grace.

> *But grow in the grace and knowledge of our Lord and Savior Jesus Christ. To him be the glory both now and to the day of eternity. Amen.*
> —2 Peter 3:18

Those who grow in truly knowing God's grace will grow in grace themselves. Again, an important distinction needs to be made: a person may know a lot *about* grace and even be able to preach good sermons about grace without ever having really experienced it.

Imagine if I studied an item on a dessert menu to the point where I could name every single ingredient used and the order in which they were combined. I could describe it to you with great accuracy and probably make good speculations about what it would be like to eat it. Now imagine how different it would be if I were to describe a dessert to you while it was in my mouth. I'd be able to tell you more than just facts about it; I could tell you my experience of it through all five senses. Which recommendation would you trust more?

In the same way, there's a visible difference between a person who knows a lot about grace and a person who has tasted it, and you will see it most clearly in the way he or she lives. People who really understand what it means to have the crushing weight of sin and death lifted from their shoulders, having done nothing to earn it, delight in sharing that grace with others. Pride and self-righteousness flee from a heart that is constantly meditating on the tender mercies of the Father.

By contrast, people who know about grace conceptually but haven't felt it applied to their own lives have no problem preaching about grace while showing none to the people around them. There's a disconnect between the knowledge and the outworking. This sort of knowledge without accompanying heart change may look closer to maturity than outright ignorance, but Jesus makes it clear in Matthew 23 how He feels about religious hypocrisy. Seriously, stop now and read that chapter of Scripture if you have any doubt about how serious this problem is.

I would urge pastors and leaders to keep this in mind as you shepherd others. Disciple people the way Jesus did, modeling the principles you teach and holding people accountable to do likewise. Similarly, for those of you who are looking for mentorship or wanting to go deeper with God, don't look for the smartest person or run straight to the classroom. Look for someone whose way of life is worthy of imitation, and follow that person as he or she follows Christ.

Another Barrier

Another reason we have failed at bringing Christians to maturity is our obsession with numbers. Many refuse to admit it, but we make a lot of decisions based on what will draw a crowd. Again, this was not the model of Christ. He made right decisions based on right priorities, and it resulted in fewer followers. Because we have not followed His model, people flock to our services who never would have followed Jesus. If you're better at gathering crowds and securing praise than Jesus was, something's off.

We have been giving the people what they want. This is why many churches stopped their prayer gatherings. People weren't interested in coming. This is why true life-on-life discipleship is rarely seen. People don't want to get that close or invest that much time. We like our space. We may do a short-term Bible study with a group, but existing as a family is asking too much. As church leaders, we figure we need to work with what we have. We don't want to lose anyone, so we have to find the lowest common denominators. If the majority of our congregation will give us only an hour on Sunday and an occasional Bible study or class, then we have to get them to maturity within those parameters.

When I planted my first church, I wanted to create a space where people could slip in and have a great encounter with God through His Word and have the freedom to slip out immediately after the service was over. I honestly had no thought of the congregation growing in their love for one another. I created a church that I wanted to attend. I figured there were a lot of busy Christians who had enough friends and came to the church to grow closer to God, not to each other. I liked my privacy, so I figured others did as well. I was right. People flooded to these gatherings, and they were exciting. However, the elders and I became very convicted about the fact that Christ wanted us known for our love for one another. Though we weren't unloving, we knew it wasn't our love that was attracting visitors.

Week after week, we were pleading with the congregation to love one another deeply, especially those who were different from them. While some caught on, many could not. I had gotten them used to a way of gathering that allowed us to keep one another at arm's length, and change would not be easy. The more we tried to force relationships, the more everyone got frustrated and many went to other churches. It was one of the most miserable times of my life. For fifteen

Too often we treat
community and discipleship as
optional add-ons that are available
for those who are interested
in that kind of thing.

years, I had experienced only numerical growth. I was used to excitement and increased attendance. Now I was watching close friends leave our church. It was a difficult time, and I wasn't certain of what God wanted me to do. Do I give the people the kind of church they want, or can I force them to become the kind of church I saw in Scripture? Do I keep pushing no matter how many people leave, or is there a point where I am sinning by my impatience? Passages like 2 Timothy 4:2 are confusing because I'm still not sure if I was supposed to "reprove, rebuke, and exhort" or if I just needed "complete patience and teaching":

> *Preach the word; be ready in season and out of season; reprove, rebuke, and exhort, with complete patience and teaching.*

Since then I have spoken to many pastors of megachurches who are in the same predicament. You feel a deep weight of responsibility for being the one to steer your congregation down a path you now believe is wrong. You've created your own opposition, and people will be quick to remind you of that. And yet, you can't in good conscience continue leading them in a way that is stunting their growth.

> *A new commandment I give to you, that you love one another: just as I have loved you, you*

also are to love one another. By this all people
will know that you are my disciples, if you have
love for one another.

                                    —John 13:34–35

This is what God wants: groups of mature believers who show the world supernatural love for each other. The love component of church is not negotiable. Too often we treat community and discipleship as optional add-ons that are available for those who are interested in that kind of thing. It's like adding avocado on your burrito—it'll make it taste better, but if it's not worth it to you, there's no need to pay extra.

That's crazy!! Love is supposed to be the point of church! Joining the church is supposed to be joining into this incredible oneness with God *and* each other. When I started Cornerstone, my goal was not this deep supernatural love. I just assumed maturity would happen if people came every week and listened to the best sermons I could deliver. I now realize that maturity has at least as much to do with relationship as knowledge. But not everyone is interested in perfect oneness with each other. There are those who are interested in "going to church" for a one-hour service but have no desire to enter into deep relationships. This makes no sense biblically! The church IS a united Body. The more mature a church becomes, the deeper their love will be. Our misunderstanding of maturity has left the church immature.

Love Is for Babies

It seems like, at least in some circles, we've started to look down on those who emphasize love as immature. As if we thought that baby Christians need to be taught about love, but eventually they should grow up and move on to more mature topics: eschatology, timing of creation, and other esoteric details. Who decided that emphasizing doctrine was mature and emphasizing love was immature? From everything I can see in the New Testament, love is not something you just move past. Consider the way Paul writes to the Thessalonian church:

> *Now may our God and Father himself, and our Lord Jesus, direct our way to you, and may the Lord make you increase and abound in love for one another and for all, as we do for you, so that he may establish your hearts blameless in holiness before our God and Father, at the coming of our Lord Jesus with all his saints.*
>
> *—1 Thessalonians 3:11–13*

> *Now concerning brotherly love you have no need for anyone to write to you, for you yourselves have been taught by God to love one another, for that indeed is what you are doing to all the*

brothers throughout Macedonia. But we urge
you, brothers, to do this more and more.

—1 Thessalonians 4:9–10

We ought always to give thanks to God for you,
brothers, as is right, because your faith is grow-
ing abundantly, and the love of every one of you
for one another is increasing.

—2 Thessalonians 1:3

It sure seems like—according to these passages, among many others—one of Paul's primary measures of maturity was love. In the first passage, Paul prays that God would cause the believers to increase and abound in love, *so that* their hearts would be blameless in holiness. Love here almost seems to be equated with sanctification! Remember the diagram above. The place where most people begin veering off the path to maturity is at the point where they must begin discipling others and walking deeply with other believers. Sanctification *depends* on relationship. It depends on love.

And this makes so much sense! Anyone who is a parent or even a spouse understands that family sanctifies you like nothing else. When you get married, all of a sudden your life is not your own. Your patience, humility, gentleness, and self-control are tested from a closer range than ever before. Flaws that are easy to mask from a distance begin to show their true colors pretty quick. Then before you know it, you have a baby, and the amount of patience and gentleness you need seems to skyrocket all over again.

We were never meant to cultivate these virtues in isolation. God has created us in such a way that we crave relationships and family. He designed the church to be a family that is *even more* devoted to one another than to their biological families (Luke 14:26; Matt. 12:46–50).

"A Still More Excellent Way"

Our job is to get people into this mind-set. In our own reasoning we think, *"People just aren't interested in this."* We're probably right. But if Jesus stated it as clearly as this—this is *the way* He said people will recognize His followers—we can't settle for what people naturally want to do.

Christians seem to want to continue learning their whole lives in a noncommittal environment where they aren't expected to actually *act* on what they've learned. Maybe so. But that can't stop us from pursuing what Jesus commands. Our highest goal can't be keeping people around. We can't compromise on discipleship.

We are so prone to forget that Jesus literally and specifically said that the two most important commands are (1) to love God and (2) to love the people around us (Matt. 22:36–40). One key part of discipleship is teaching people statements like this. The other crucial element is teaching people to live as though this teaching were true.

When we equate maturity with knowledge, it's easy to justify a life spent acquiring knowledge and finding fault with others. There are of course biblical commands to avoid false doctrine and instructions to correct those who teach something other than God's truth. Those passages are numerous, and we need to take them seriously. But they can't be taken in isolation.

The Bible gives many *more* commands to love others, to be united with others, to avoid quarreling and division, and to promote peace. They need to be taken seriously. Literally, even. But they require something of us. Living in love is what *actual* maturity looks like. Because love "rejoices with the truth" (1 Cor. 13:6), mature love will include zeal for doctrinal truth. But that love will find ways to not just speak about but actually *be* kind, patient, not envious, not boastful, not arrogant, not rude, and all the other traits of love.

This road to maturity requires much greater depths of sacrifice, investment, and effort. "For the gate is narrow and the way is hard that leads to life, and those who find it are few" (Matt. 7:14). But, just like having a family, the rewards are unparalleled.

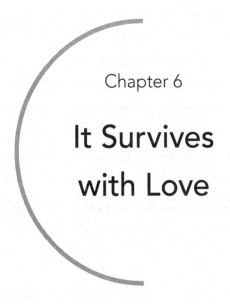

Chapter 6

It Survives
with Love

Love Is the Answer

Is it possible to value theology, hate sin, and fight for unity? If so, we have very few examples of this. The people who want unity often have a "can't we all just get along" attitude that downplays the seriousness of good theology and a holy lifestyle. Since God commands all three, there must be a way to grow in our theology, holiness, and unity simultaneously.

It might sound oversimplified and cheesy, but love is the answer.

Our divisions usually aren't caused by a difference in theology but a lack of relationship. Our problem is not our difference of opinion or interpretation; it's the shallowness of our "love." Our love, if we can even call it that, is not born from rich theology that reminds us of the spiritual reality that we are one Body. Most would affirm this truth, but we've never taken the time to meditate on it and internalize it.

When you're deeply in love, division is unfathomable. I can't imagine a situation where it would be easier for me to leave my wife than to work through the issue. I love her too much. To distance from her would be devastating.

In the church, we divide easily because we love shallowly.

Not to belabor the point, but I can't imagine ever telling Lisa that it would be easier if I just took three of the kids and started a new family. She in turn could keep the house, the four other kids and just keep her family going. I know this happens all the time when love fades, and that's my point. In our case, after twenty-seven years of marriage, our love has only grown deeper. Each year it's more difficult to imagine being apart from her. Each year I believe we are capable of surviving even greater conflicts together. Our arguments become more tame over the years because we both value being together more than we value being right.

Who Are We Kidding

It's easy to spot real love. Sometimes it's in a person's expressions or body language. Sometimes the obsession shows itself by constant affirmation or sacrifice. It's obvious when someone deeply loves his girlfriend, wife, or child. It's also quite apparent to those around when that love isn't there and a relationship is obligatory. My point is that we really aren't fooling anyone with our forced greeting times at church or our sermons and songs about Christian love. When love is lacking, it almost makes it worse that we keep talking about it because we shouldn't need to. I doubt Jesus went around telling everyone how much He loved His disciples. Everyone knew. It was obvious. Instead of improving our speech and nuancing, we need to beg for a change of heart.

Despite our words, our lack of true love is clear to the rest of the world. Our theological pride has created divisions that run deep. The only ones who can't see this are the ones who don't want to. Our annoyance over each other's sin is equally obvious. We can try to mask it as grief and concern, but the world sees it for what it most often is: self-righteousness and eagerness to judge. It's very difficult nowadays to find anyone outside the church who actually admires the church. The best a non-Christian will give us is, "I'm glad you found something that works for you." We are light-years from the love that shows the world we have been discipled by Jesus.

The Dream

Imagine walking into a room where there wasn't a single person thinking of himself or herself, including you. In humility, they all considered others more important than themselves. It's not a shallow, forced selflessness. It's really who they are. They are all so overwhelmed by the love of God that they have no want. They don't just say encouraging things to you, but you can tell that deep inside they really feel it. They genuinely love you and have been praying for you throughout the week. Everyone works his or her way throughout the room, blessing everyone he or she sees. God has given some of them specific words of encouragement or exhortation for you. Others are reading Scriptures to you or praying for you. Some might have physical gifts that the Holy Spirit told them to give you as they were in prayer for you that week.

It's more than a family. Everyone treats the others like they are members of the same body. We grieve together, celebrate together. There isn't a person in the room who wouldn't give his or her life for you. There isn't a family who wouldn't open up their home to you if you were in need. Rich or poor, no one viewed their possessions as belonging to themselves. Everyone was a giver. There is no gossip, ungodly judging, or fighting. They live like one body.

God is clearly in your midst, and miracles start taking place. The deep love results in God releasing power from

Heaven. Your friends are cured of sickness and ailments. Unbelievers encounter Christ for the first time. Words of knowledge and prophecy are spoken. The greatest miracle is the joy and peace that everyone feels in the presence of God. You bask in the joy of knowing this is not just a gathering. This is life. This is your tribe, family, church.

Imagine knowing there were groups like this all around the world. You have brothers and sisters, Body members, in every country. You can go to any of these groups and experience the same oneness and mutual sacrifice. You have family all over the earth. The happiest people on the planet, totally secure in their oneness with God, loving you as you love them. All your fears turn to complete security. You always knew that God promised to provide for you, but now you see His Body promising you the same thing.

I used to wonder if this could ever happen on this earth, but now I've seen glimpses of it. Before you get disappointed that your church does not live this way, ask yourself if you do.

The Nightmare

Two years ago, I spoke at an event. I'll spare you all the details, but the time I spent with this group was special. My time with the Lord was unique as I fellowshipped with this group. Their leader was like no other leader I had met. His humility was different. It wasn't forced. He wasn't trying to sound humble; he just was. He was an example to me, and still is to this day. I kept thinking of the scene in John 1:47 "Jesus saw Nathanael coming to him, and said of him, 'Behold an Israelite indeed, in whom is no deceit!'" He didn't seem to have any selfish ambition as he was leading large groups into true discipleship. His knowledge of the Word was exemplary, and his love for people was evident. In short, he reminded me a lot of Jesus. We began serving together at different events, and God did unique things through us every time we were together.

Then came the conflict.

A couple of my staff approached me one day and asked, "Did you know that his organization is strongly egalitarian? In fact, they even wrote a book about it." We started to question whether our partnership could move forward. If we were both training Christian leaders, how could one of us teach that God wants men and women to be elders in the church while the other taught that the role of the elder is reserved for men? We both seemed to have searched the Scriptures thoroughly, and neither of us seemed to have a selfish agenda, yet we came to different interpretations of the same biblical texts. My immediate response was to do what most of us do in these situations: practice social distancing. Admit that we are both Christian, graciously part ways, affirm a friendship, but keep each other at arm's length from here on out. That

In the church, we divide easily

because we love shallowly.

tends to be the easiest way to maintain Christian unity and avoid the conflict from escalating.

Something was biblically off in taking that path, however, and I didn't feel peace about it for two reasons. (1) I am commanded by Jesus to love my brother as Christ loves me. Jesus has not kept me at a safe distance but keeps pursuing a deeper love. (2) I don't see this theological disagreement as something that warrants separation.

Maybe there was a deeper reason for my discomfort toward the idea of separating from this leader than the lack of biblical logic for it. There was a true love between us, so it wasn't easy to part ways. We saw God do things uniquely when we ministered together. He had shown us that we were better serving together. The more we talked about the issues, the more we thought that even this disagreement might be a Kingdom blessing. If we figured out how to pursue unity rather than distancing in our disagreement, maybe God could use us as an example.

A few months later we found ourselves in Myanmar, each of us taking members of ministries to serve together in reaching people who had never heard of Jesus. We committed to pursuing oneness and began to experience the "good and pleasant" benefits of unity described in Psalm 133. One of his leaders pointed out verse 3, which states "For there the LORD has commanded the blessing, life forevermore." Not only will we experience the joy of unity, but God will command blessing in that kind of relationship. And that is exactly what we experienced over the next few days.

I have believed that miracles of healing were possible, and I have believed the testimonies of friends who had experienced them. I just had never seen it with my own eyes, until that trip. I never watched Him use me as the vehicle for His healing. I was actually present as deaf kids heard for the first time. I was the one who had the honor of laying hands on people and watching pain go away and swelling disappear. Most importantly, I saw people who had never even heard of Jesus begin to embrace Him. Without exaggerating, those were the best days of my life. I believe there was something about the pursuit of unity amid theological differences coupled with a pursuit of the unreached that resulted in the blessing.

When Theology Should Divide Us

Some of you are reading this right now and thinking that it sounds alright in theory, but what happens when someone's interpretation appears to be a complete contradiction of Scripture? Am I supposed to pursue unity at all costs? The answer to that is no. Doctrinal precision on primary issues is vital. Paul said that anyone preaching a different gospel should be cursed (Gal. 1:8)! He spells out the gospel in 1 Corinthians 15:1–8. Deviating from or distorting this cannot be tolerated. Just as there is a time when sin should divide, there is also a time when false teachers must be removed from the Church.

> *For many deceivers have gone out into the world, those who do not confess the coming of Jesus Christ in the flesh. Such a one is the deceiver and the antichrist. Watch yourselves, so that you may not lose what we have worked for, but may win a full reward. Everyone who goes on ahead and does not abide in the teaching of Christ, does not have God. Whoever abides in the teaching has both the Father and the Son. If anyone comes to you and does not bring this teaching, do not receive him into your house or give him any greeting, for whoever greets him takes part in his wicked works.*
>
> —2 John 7–11

John is warning the believers that there are "deceivers" who will be spreading their false teachings. Here he cites their denial of "the coming of Jesus Christ in the flesh." Rather than teaching the same things that Jesus taught while He was on earth, they deny that He ever came in the flesh. John is explicit in that we need to steer far from those who do not "abide in the teaching of Christ." We are to seek teachers who by evidence of their teaching and lifestyle abide in Christ and refuse to receive those who don't abide in His teachings.

I have seen this passage used by modern-day heresy hunters to encourage the removal of anyone who doesn't adhere to any theological position they hold. I would just like to caution you that John is speaking of the extreme and specific case here of people who denied that Christ came in the flesh. It's not about just any point of theology.

Remember that Paul told the Corinthians "I decided to know nothing among you except Jesus Christ and him crucified" (1 Cor. 2:2). Does that mean he didn't care about or teach on anything else? Of course not! But the writers of the New Testament had a clear concern over key beliefs regarding Jesus.

Here are a few of the false teachings warned against in the New Testament:

- Claiming "I am the Christ" (Matt. 24:5)
- Saying "Jesus is accursed" (1 Cor. 12:3)
- Judging people over the foods they eat and festivals they celebrate, requiring harsh bodily discipline as a means of attaining godliness (Col. 2:16–23)
- Getting caught up in "myths and endless genealogies, which promote speculations" (1 Tim. 1:4)

- Forbidding marriage and certain foods
  (1 Tim. 4:3)
- Wandering off into "myths" (2 Tim. 4:4)
- Denying that Jesus came in the flesh
  (1 John 4:1–3; 2 John 7)
- Turning the grace of God into sensuality
  (Jude 4)

We're talking about key gospel truths here, more in line with Paul's "know[ing] nothing among you except Jesus Christ and him crucified" than with beliefs about end times or the correct usage of spiritual gifts or social reform or the mode of baptism or the precise nature of the Lord's Supper. Again, I'm not saying that beliefs on all these things aren't important. But I am suggesting that we've taken the biblical category of "false teacher" and started to apply it to anyone who disagrees with us on virtually anything. That's slander!

This doesn't mean we don't challenge each other's actions or teachings, but we must do it with love and humility, seeking their repentance. Paul confronted Peter directly when he observed that Peter's "conduct was not in step with the truth of the gospel"—interestingly because by his behavior he was encouraging division between Jews and Gentiles in the Body (Gal. 2:11–14). This loving confrontation is vital! We can't be soft on truth. But we have to pursue truth in the same way that Jesus and the apostles did.

Partnership without Compromise

Unity doesn't require that we compromise on our own convictions. Paul tells the Romans that "each one should be fully convinced in his own mind"(14:5). He goes on to explain that each person is going to be judged by God, so each one must be careful to obey the Scriptures according to his or her best understanding of them. In this passage, Paul says some things which at first glance sound relativistic. I challenge you to pray with full faith that the Holy Spirit is with you, meditate on these verses, and see what God reveals to you.

> *Therefore let us not pass judgment on one another any longer, but rather decide never to put a stumbling block or hindrance in the way of a brother. I know and am persuaded in the Lord Jesus that nothing is unclean in itself, but it is unclean for anyone who thinks it unclean. For if your brother is grieved by what you eat, you are no longer walking in love. By what you eat, do not destroy the one for whom*

Christ died. So do not let what you regard as good be spoken of as evil. For the kingdom of God is not a matter of eating and drinking but of righteousness and peace and joy in the Holy Spirit. Whoever thus serves Christ is acceptable to God and approved by men. So then let us pursue what makes for peace and for mutual upbuilding.

—Romans 14:13–19

At first glance, Paul sounds a lot like the people in our culture who commonly say, "I'm glad it works for you, but I have my own truth." After all, Paul is saying that two people can eat the same thing, yet it might be right for one and wrong for the other. However, Paul is not teaching relativity. He is explaining that there is an absolute truth: "nothing is unclean in itself." He then shows that there is more to being right in God's eyes than knowing the correct answer. We can be technically correct yet terribly sinful.

God is not just looking for the right answer but the right love and priorities.

Let's approach this passage with reverence. We can't belittle or overreact to it. Paul's underlying fear of God is woven throughout this passage. He has just reminded these Christians that they will each give an account before God.

Each phrase is a word from the Lord, so let's treat it as such. Take some time to look at every single phrase of this passage. For now, I just want to point out a few phrases that you may have skimmed but never digested.

"It is unclean for anyone who thinks it unclean."
Paul's point is that if someone is still uncertain of a biblical principle, you can lead that person into sin by pushing him or her to do something that he or she doesn't yet have a clear conscience about before God.

"If your brother is grieved by what you eat, you are no longer walking in love."
Don't move past this too quickly. There is a priority given toward walking in love that we need to internalize. Paul is warning of a danger that can quickly creep into any of our lives. We can be so focused on our debates that we lose sight of love.

"By what you eat, do not destroy the one for whom Christ died."
Meditate on "the one for whom Christ died." It is so healthy to meditate on Christ's love toward specific individuals. It reminds us of His feelings toward these people. He loved them enough to die for them. Internalizing that truth might overcome our irritation and indifference.

"The kingdom of God is not a matter of eating and drinking but of righteousness and peace and joy in the Holy Spirit.

The Kingdom is about "righteousness and peace and joy in the Holy Spirit." Improper use of our "knowledge" can actually pull people away from these things and cause them to focus on lesser issues.

"Whoever thus serves Christ is acceptable to God."

It's not a matter of finding the right answer to the question of what's acceptable to eat. If we're serving Christ in righteousness and peace and joy in the Holy Spirit, then we are acceptable to God. What standard of orthodoxy could we add to this that would be more important than someone being declared "acceptable to God"?

"Let us pursue what makes for peace and for mutual upbuilding."

The goal is peace and edification. It seems we often let our goal slip to correctness and exclusion.

We have to stop assuming that everyone who is right with God will look, act, and think exactly like us. There should be freedom among shepherds to watch over their flocks in the manner they feel right about before God. I am not saying this will be an easy road, but I am saying that we will be surprised at how resolutions are found when love is central.

One Body, One Spirit

In Ephesians 4, Paul writes that we should "*walk in a manner worthy of the calling to which you have been called, with all humility and gentleness, with patience, bearing with one another in love, eager to maintain the unity of the Spirit in the bond of peace*" (vv. 1–3). Notice that he doesn't say we need to create or cultivate the unity of the Spirit but to *maintain* it.

He follows that up by writing that "there is *one* body and *one* Spirit."

In his book *The Normal Christian Church Life*, Watchman Nee wrote a chapter on the basis of union and division. According to him, the basis on which we accept or reject any person to the family of God has to be whether or not that person has the Holy Spirit. In his words:

> How are we going to determine who are our brothers and our fellow members in the Church of God? Not by inquiring if they hold the same doctrinal views that we hold, or have had the same spiritual experiences; nor by seeing if their customs, manner of living, interests, and preferences tally with ours. We merely inquire, Are they indwelt by the Spirit of God or not? We cannot insist

> on oneness of opinions, or oneness of experi-
> ence, or any other oneness among believers,
> except the oneness of the Spirit. That oneness
> there can be, and always must be, among the
> children of God. All who have this oneness
> are in the Church.[5]

Ultimately, we do not get to determine who is called a child of God—He does. And the sign that He gives to confirm someone's salvation is the indwelling of the Holy Spirit.

We see this play out with the early church in Acts 10–11, when Peter has his vision of the sheet of "unclean" animals coming down from Heaven. Just after, Peter is instructed to go to the house of a Gentile believer. He preaches to him and his household, and the Holy Spirit falls on them. When Peter returns to Jerusalem, he is met with opposition and criticism from the Jewish believers because he spent time with uncircumcised Gentiles. In his defense, Peter tells them of the Holy Spirit falling on the Gentiles. Acts 11:18 relates: "When they heard these things they fell silent. And they glorified God, saying, 'Then to the Gentiles also God has granted repentance that leads to life.'" There was a reverence for the Holy Spirit at that time to the point where even though it went against all their cultural norms and

If you are willing
to let the presence of
the Spirit take precedence ...
you will find a much more diverse,
beautiful family of believers
because it is the family that
God has made, not the one
you have chosen.

deep-seated beliefs, they *could not* call unclean what God had deemed pure.

We have to be extremely careful not to take the place of the Holy Spirit in the name of discernment or wisdom. You can be sure that God will not take lightly the defamation of one of His children. I have seven children now. Can you imagine how absurd it would be to me if six of them got together and decided to excommunicate one of their siblings from the family? No matter how many arguments or differences my kids have, they will always be family because they have the same DNA.

Too often, we have made doctrine the crux of our evaluations of other believers over and above the presence of the Holy Spirit. I know I have. If you are willing to let the presence of the Spirit take precedence over exact theological alignment in secondary issues, I believe you will find a much more diverse, beautiful family of believers because it is the family that God has made, not the one you have chosen.

The Real Prodigal

One way to consider the concept of unity is to imagine that God is calling all of us to join Him at a table for a meal. After all the heartbreak and rebellion and doubts and struggle, the Bible ends with a picture of God's people joining Him for a marriage feast. Even now, the table is open, and God's work in this world consists of drawing us in to sit and eat.

In Jesus' parable of the prodigal son (Luke 15:11–32), one son runs off to spend his portion of his inheritance while the other son stays at home with their father. When the young prodigal returns home in shame, the father runs to embrace and restore him while the older brother pouts outside and refuses to join the party his father throws to celebrate the son's return.

We tend to focus on the sons in this story, but we should ask: What is the father's goal for each of his sons? To get them to sit down together with him at the table! What are each of the sons resisting in his own way? Sitting down for the family meal.

Why the table?

It's a place of celebration. A place of relationship. A place of healing. Of mutuality. Of equality. Grace. Blessing.

The two sons are invited to join their father at a table. Not a classroom. Not a temple. What the father was after was not education or ritual. He was after relationship. It wasn't about what they could offer. It was about *them*.

One version of immaturity and one source of disunity is running away from the Father to pursue our own passions. When we are able to get past the madness that drives us to the far country in search of pleasure or significance or autonomy, we can set aside all our shame and come back to the Father just as we are. We can stop trying to live large or make a name for ourselves. We can stop running from the relationship we know deep down will be the purest and most meaningful we will ever experience.

The Father is calling: "Come home. Join me at the table. It's time to celebrate."

But the other version of immaturity and source of disunity is standing there like the religious older brother, who refused to join the party because the younger brother sinned. When we are able to release our outrage that the prodigal has returned, to stop demanding penance or some positive contribution from our brothers (or sisters) who have failed, we can set aside all our self-righteousness and come back to the Father just as we are. In these moments, we know that we and all our siblings belong at the table. There is no one we want to see excluded. We acknowledge that the table was made for *this*. We let go of our longing to celebrate accomplishments, and we instead long to celebrate *people*. And our love for them leads us to first accept the Father's invitation to the table and then to stand beside Him as He invites the prodigal to the feast.

The Father is calling: "Come home. Join me at the table. It's time to celebrate."

Regardless of your past or current sins, you're invited to God's table. But eating means celebrating. And actually, the feast is a celebration that *everyone* is at the table again. You don't get to celebrate only yourself or only your favorites. The feast flows out of the Father's joy—we get to share in His joy. And His joy is over the gathering of all His children, including the ones who have not cleaned themselves up and those who nearly refused to come because of their disgust over the guest list. They all belong at this table. Celebrating means eating and drinking *together*. As *equals*. It's more than a handshake or a contract. It's a party. The point is to enjoy being together.

Remember 1 John. It's not maintaining the line of doctrinal precision that makes us true children of God. It's whether or not we've received His love, whether or not we keep His commandments, and whether or not His love flows from us to the people around us. How different would the Church look today if instead of whispered gossipy exchanges we actually sat down at a table, looked each other in the eyes, and enjoyed the relationship? Celebrated it?

The feast will happen with or without us. The question is whether our disapproval of the guest list will keep us from joining our brothers and sisters. And our Father.

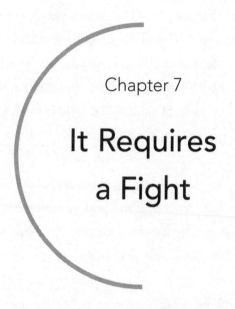

Chapter 7

It Requires a Fight

"Blessed are the peacemakers, for they
shall be called sons of God."

Matthew 5:9

Peacemakers love unity and by nature hate conflict. The problem is that unity will never happen without a fight. We can't forget that we have an Enemy, and he exists to deceive and create division. Satan wants us separated from God and each other. He isn't going to just sit back and allow a movement of unity to take place in the church. If it's ever going to happen, it will require a fight. And this usually doesn't come naturally for a peacemaker.

Don't forget that Jesus was the greatest peacemaker. He made peace between God and us. Despite being known for bringing peace, He had some harsh words for the religious leaders of His day. This isn't a contradiction. Satan planted leaders amid the people of God to take their focus off the commands and priorities of God.

> *Woe to you, scribes and Pharisees, hypocrites! For you tithe mint and dill and cumin, and have neglected the weightier matters of the law: justice and mercy and faithfulness. These you ought to have done, without neglecting the others. You blind guides, straining out a gnat and swallowing a camel!*
>
> —Matthew 23:23–24

Jesus is clear: not all issues are equal. There are "weightier" matters. Just as He declared the greatest command at the end of the previous chapter, He now emphasizes the priorities of justice, mercy, and faithfulness. Notice that He makes His point about showing mercy while speaking some pretty abrasive words against the religious leaders. In fact, He seems to make a sarcastic remark that would have shamed those leaders. He reminds us there is an appropriate time to overturn tables and make strong statements against those who emphasize the wrong things.

We need to confront with caution because we don't have the same discernment as Jesus. At the same time, our goal in life is to walk as Jesus walked. This means there is a time to speak boldly. When God's people are mistreated or God's house is being denigrated, staying silent becomes sinful.

Fight against Division

After four chapters of demanding that believers end their divisions, Paul starts chapter 5 of 1 Corinthians requiring that they remove certain people from their gatherings. We will never have the unity that God wants of His Bride if we allow certain people to remain in our circle. Far from being a loveless act, the church's love is dependent on its ability to challenge errant theology, confront unrepentant sin, and remove those who cause unnecessary divisions. Every day, new individuals start ministries, wrongfully dividing the Body of Christ. They may be accurate in their theological assessment, but that doesn't make their slander acceptable.

Just as we need to be extremely cautious not to damage those who are a part of the Body, we have to be just as cautious to remove certain individuals from the church because of the damage they will do by remaining.

But now I am writing to you not to associate
with anyone who bears the name of brother if
he is guilty of sexual immorality or greed, or is
an idolater, reviler, drunkard, or swindler—
not even to eat with such a one. For what have
I to do with judging outsiders? Is it not those
inside the church whom you are to judge? God
judges those outside. "Purge the evil person from
among you."

—1 Corinthians 5:11–13

Passages like 1 Corinthians 5 are difficult for many to digest because we live in a culture that minimizes the seriousness of sin and misunderstands grace. Many take Christ's command of "judge not" and apply it to every situation, even though Paul clearly commands us to judge people who call themselves "brother." Paul just told the church "do not pronounce judgment before the time, before the Lord comes, who will bring to light the things now hidden in darkness" (4:5). Now he commands us to judge those inside the church. It may sound contradictory, but we know that it can't be.

Jesus addressed those who judged others and by so doing felt like they themselves were not subject to judgment.

Judge not, that you be not judged. For with the judgment you pronounce you will be judged, and with the measure you use it will be measured to you.

—Matthew 7:1–2

He is correcting the attitude of those who are so busy looking at the small faults of others that they are blinded to the glaring sin in their own lives. It's a serious warning for those who are in any position of authority. In exercising our authority, we can forget that we are still under a far higher authority. In context, Jesus is not saying that we universally should never judge. In fact, Jesus was also clear that there is a time to remove people from your fellowship. In Matthew 18:15–20, Jesus speaks about the unrepentant person who gathers with the believers. He prescribes a loving process by which the church should seek the person's repentance. However, if he or she refuses to listen to a loving believer, a group of believers, and even an entire congregation, that person must no longer be accepted as a believer.

Many think that removing a person from a church sounds unloving. On the contrary, this is not just for the church's benefit but for the benefit of the wayward individual as well.

When you are assembled in the name of the Lord
Jesus and my spirit is present, with the power of
our Lord Jesus, you are to deliver this man to
Satan for the destruction of the flesh, so that his
spirit may be saved in the day of the Lord.
                                        —1 Corinthians 5:4–5

How in the world can "deliver this man to Satan" be a loving act? You only have to look at the goal: "so that his spirit may be saved in the day of the Lord." Paul is mindful of Judgment Day. He is concerned about this person's eternal destiny. The hope of removing unrepentant people from fellowship and delivering them to Satan is for their eternal good. By removing them from the authority, fellowship, and care of a loving congregation and handing them over to the authority of Satan, we are hoping they find the emptiness and dissatisfaction of remaining in sin. The hope is that they taste the absence of church fellowship and realize that sin and Satan don't compare.

As their flesh is destroyed by their sin, the goal is that they would come running back to the church.

Notice that this is not about a person who is struggling with sin and frequently turning in repentance back to God. This is about a person who engages in sin and refuses to acknowledge his or her sin to God and the Christian community.

I'm guessing that 99 percent of churchgoers in America would never participate in what they perceive to be a cruel act and believe that they have a better method than Jesus and Paul. There are some who will never be convinced that the removal of someone who claims to be Christian is the right thing to do. I would just encourage you to consider the possibility that though your position is currently most popular, it might not be most biblical. A general practice in my life is that whenever my methodology differs from that of Christ, I assume that His method is better.

Fight for Others

Something we learn at a young age is that it's always easier to be critical. It's the cool kids who can make fun of others to show their superiority. If you dare stand up for someone being bullied, you run the risk of being the next target. It's always safer to be on the critical side: speaking negatively about teachers, parents, or peers. The same is true in the church today. Try standing up for a Christian leader you think was mistreated. Worse yet, try showing encouragement to someone who misspoke or fell into sin. Our church culture makes it very difficult to make positive comments about any Christian leader. Negative comments draw louder praise and softer criticism. Fewer and fewer people dare speak up in favor of their brothers and sisters, while attacking voices are growing in number and volume.

Every leader has a group of critics ready to pounce on those who support him or her. I have received emails and phone calls threatening me that if I don't take back kind statements I have made about certain people, I would become the next target. It feels like middle school all over again. Do I distance myself from certain brothers and sisters so I can sit at the table with the cool kids? Or do I refuse to abandon people once I am certain that I see the Spirit in them? Or I could go with the option that several have literally suggested to me: hang out with them but not in public and never affirm them in any way publicly. I'm sure some of you think I'm exaggerating at this point. I wish I was.

It's a tough time to be a Christian leader. It has never been easy, but it's never been this hard. That's not necessarily a bad thing. As Paul was suffering for sharing the gospel, he was also suffering attacks from within the church. He wrote 2 Corinthians to encourage the church to stand with him rather than against him, and he makes a powerful statement in the first chapter:

> *Indeed, we felt that we had received the sentence of death. But that was to make us rely not on ourselves but on God who raises the dead.*
>
> —2 Corinthians 1:9

The Lord in His
sovereignty chose for us to
live in this time, so we must
trust that He will give us grace
to navigate through this with
strength and love.

The most painful times in life force us to rely on the God of resurrection. Paul saw that as a good thing, and we should also. From this, you can argue that Christian leaders need to toughen up. They shouldn't become so easily discouraged, depressed, and suicidal. Maybe you're right, but did God really intend it to be this way? I speak to many pastors who are hanging on by a thread or have already given up. It's like they are getting jabbed left and right by people leaving the faith, sin increasing in their cities, divorces, depression, addictions, their own temptations and family struggles, financial hardships, being compared to better leaders and teachers, and the like. But then comes the knockout punch: the people who were supposed to be in their corner take a swing.

My point is not to make you feel sorry for Christian leaders. There will always be those who can take any abuse and see it as a good thing, an opportunity to *rely not on ourselves but on God who raises the dead.* My point is that it doesn't have to be this way, and it's for your benefit and the benefit of the church's future if we fight for unity. What if leaders viewed the church like they view God: as the place they could always run to?

The news has been affecting me differently lately. When I hear of Christian leaders committing suicide, having affairs, or leaving the faith, I wonder what I am doing or not doing that adds to the problem. Could I have made a difference?

Has my unwillingness to fight for Christian unity resulted in more and more people assuming it will never happen? Could things have been different if the church really became a group that exuded supernatural love?

A couple of years ago, I wrote an article to help Christian leaders respond well to those who have criticized them, and I want to share some of those thoughts here. We typically either fight back with the wrong attitude or we get discouraged and don't respond at all. The Bible teaches us how to respond in a godly, loving, and firm way that can bring the church closer to unity.

Responding to Christian Trolls

Some of us pastors remember doing ministry before cell phones and the internet. If someone wanted to confront you, they would have to physically find you. And if they wanted to gain a following, they would have to know people. Those days are long gone. We now live in a time when strangers can write anything about you and immediately gather an audience. In fact, the more extreme the accusation, the more attention they will receive. We can't allow ourselves to get angry about this. The Lord in His sovereignty chose for us to live in this time, so we must trust that He will give us grace to navigate through this with strength and love. Here are some things I have learned that may be helpful to you.

First, don't overreact.

I have heard some leaders get angry at those who confront false doctrine. Statements like "I can't stand the arrogance of those Reformed conservatives who think they are put on earth to judge the rest of us" don't really help the situation. Having come from the world of Reformed conservatives myself, I can assure you that there are some who are humble lovers of Christ and full of grace and power. These are much needed in the Body of Christ.

It can be frustrating to see the sheer number of heresy hunters, each one genuinely believing his or her interpretation of Scripture is most accurate. However, don't forget God's command that we cannot say to any part of the Body "I don't need you." Biblical accuracy is important. Part of the role of an elder is to refute false doctrine. I'm not saying that everyone who starts a blog or podcast claiming to save the world from false teachers is a blessing or even a believer. I'm just saying that we need people in the Body with the courage to fight for truth, even though we will all make mistakes doing so. Thank God for people who still care about absolute truth in an age when anything goes.

Second, remember your own failures.

Maybe this is more pertinent to me, as I spent years believing that a charismatic theologian was an oxymoron and anyone who called himself Catholic was going to Hell. What is ironic is that I have befriended some people who call themselves "charismatic Catholics," who trust completely in the shed blood of Christ for their salvation and are avid students of God's Word. This doesn't mean there aren't plenty of charismatics who belittle Scripture in preference to their own visions, and people who call themselves Catholic who belittle the supremacy of Christ. I'm just saying that I used to make arrogant blanket statements about entire groups of people, and God continues to correct me.

In my pride, there was a time when I sarcastically slandered people to whom I have now apologized. Sometimes I was flat-out wrong about them. Other times, I was right (at least I think so), but I had no love toward them as I questioned their theology. Remembering my own mistakes helps me show grace toward those I perceive to be in the wrong.

Third, never stop loving.

We are commanded: "bless those who curse you" (Luke 6:28). Jesus tells us we are acting like unbelievers when we return evil for evil We never have the right to stop loving, especially those who call themselves Christians. It's by our gracious response to everyone that people will see us as His children (Matt 5:44–47).

Be careful! We had better not pray that line in the Lord's Prayer, "Forgive us our trespasses, AS we forgive those who trespass against us," while harboring unforgiveness. The last thing you want is for God to hold back His grace due to your lack of humility and forgiveness.

Remember that His commands lead to life. It's always easier to remain angry, but obedience leads to greater life. I remember a time I spent an entire day fasting and praying for a guy who posted lies about me. Statements like "F*** you Francis Chan" are difficult to read from people you love. Lest you think too highly of me, rest assured that thoughts of revenge came first. Anger and hurt were the first things I felt, and it was only by the grace of God that the Holy Spirit called me to pray, fast, and love. The result was incomprehensible peace, which is often what is lacking in times of attack. God commands us to pray, and sometimes it feels like it's more for our sake than theirs.

Fourth, don't pay too much attention to the wrong things.
As a kid, I loved watching *Monday Night Football*. I remember one game where some guy ran onto the field in the middle of the game. I laughed as the police chased him down. The person was laughing when he was caught because he didn't care. He did it to get attention, and he got it from millions. Guess what happened the next week? A different guy realized he could get the same attention the same way. Then week after week, the outfits got crazier and the people did more outrageous things on the field. After several weeks, the

network decided to turn the cameras away whenever someone ran onto the field. Guess what happened? People stopped
running onto the field.

We can learn something from ABC television. People
will use any means to gain attention, and sometimes the
healthiest thing to do is to ignore them. When we engage, it
often does more harm. To quote a modern philosopher:

> "Look, if I shoot you, I'm brainless
> But if you shoot me, then you're famous"[6]
> —JAY-Z

Paul says basically the same thing, but it didn't rhyme:

> *As for a person who stirs up division, after
> warning him once and then twice, have nothing
> more to do with him.*
>   —Titus 3:10

Fifth, don't quit.
Don't stop preaching, and don't become soft in your preaching. The natural reaction is to respond by shrinking back in
fear. It can feel overwhelming when the very people attacking you are the ones who are supposed to support you. It can
result in a "screw you all, I quit" attitude. Don't go there. Be
steadfast. It will all be worth it one day.

Don't go soft. Some will become so concerned about criticism that they will only preach things that are "safe." I heard one preacher make a great statement: "Some of you are preaching for the absence of criticism rather than the presence of the Holy Spirit." So true! Don't do it! This wasn't supposed to be easy. Keep being led by the Spirit.

It's true that James teaches us to be careful because teachers will be judged more strictly. Just remember that he also says that "if anyone does not stumble in what he says, he is a perfect man" (3:2). You are going to make mistakes. You will misspeak. All of us walk away from conversations wishing we had responded differently. It's just harder for those who make those mistakes when a camera is running.

Sixth, turn your eyes upon Jesus.

Sometimes I spend too much time thinking about accusations and it crowds out the mind space that could be used meditating on God's glory (Ps. 34:1; Phil. 4:8). This is a downward spiral that Satan loves. Don't let the Enemy lie to you. You are able right now to take your eyes off any problem and worship His Majesty.

Read the story of the Pharisee and the tax collector in Luke 18:9–14. It was the Pharisee who looked down at everyone else. His mistake was not just in looking down at the tax collector but the fact that he had to take his eyes off God in order to do so. We hurt ourselves and those we are trying to impact when we take our eyes off Him for too long. Why would you want to anyway?

Seventh, believe that it does get easier.
I remember the first time it happened. I was devastated. I was the pastor of Cornerstone Church in Simi Valley. It was a church that my wife and I planted. At that time I'd led the congregation for about ten years. We had grown to thousands and decided to build a bigger facility. We purchased land, but then I got convicted. As I thought about all the starving and suffering people I met around the world, I had a hard time spending millions on a building. The thought occurred to me that we lived in Southern California, so let's forgo a building and just meet out on the grass. Then we could give all that money to people in need.

The congregation eventually supported the idea, and a reporter from the local paper came and interviewed me. It was an exciting time. The church was getting fired up, and now the world was going to hear about our church members being willing to sacrifice for the poor. Imagine how sick I felt the next day when I read the headline "Local Pastor Tries to Skirt the Law." I was tricked. The whole article was about the land we bought, and it was accusing me of destroying the environment and bringing crowds to an area that wasn't yet zoned for assemblies. It was a cry for people to stop me from requesting a special use permit for that area, but the reporter did so by accusing me of trying to break the law. This happened during the time when news articles were first placed online and people were allowed to comment. I got more and more discouraged and angry as I read comment after comment. The more vicious the comment, the sadder and sicker I felt.

An unwarranted attack can hurt deeply. But I can tell you that it does get easier if you respond graciously. I eventually sent the reporter a gift certificate to a restaurant, since I was commanded by God to do good to those who hate. That didn't take away all the pain, but obedience is always the better route. By now I have been accused of many things. I was labeled a "poverty gospel preacher" because I downsized my house and gave away too much money. Recently I was labeled a "prosperity gospel preacher" because I preached at an event where someone else was labeled a prosperity gospel guy. I kind of pride myself on being one of the few people accused of both poverty and prosperity preaching. I've been called "ultra-Reformed," "hypercharismatic," "Bible-thumping," and "judgmental." Some say I'm part of the New Apostolic Reformation (whatever that is); others say that I'm Catholic. Some say I'm a universalist, while others accuse me of thinking that I'm the Messiah. It's an interesting time we live in.

During one of the recent barrages, I was telling my wife that I was so happy because it didn't affect me like it used to. I was rejoicing because I realized that God used it all to strengthen me. While anger and revenge used to be the first response, peace and love came much more naturally this time around.

Fight for Diversity

We have talked a lot about the dangers of allowing theology to divide. If you get to the point of being able to lay aside exact theological alignment in secondary issues, you will find there are still plenty of obstacles to unity. The Enemy even uses good things to deepen the divisions. He loves to manipulate godly men and women who are stirred to fight against different evils in the world. Satan can take their anger toward evil and divert it toward fellow believers who don't fight for the same causes as passionately. Within the beautifully diverse family of God, people will affiliate with different political parties and fight for different social issues than you do. Whether it's the Black Lives Matter movement, climate change, social distancing, or whatever new issue has come to the forefront by the time you are reading this, new reasons to divide are constantly coming up.

Why Don't They Care like I Do?

Regarding such movements, I don't want to quench anyone's passion. People do this to me, and it is annoying. You step out in faith only to be met with Christians who try to calm you down rather than help. All I'm asking you to do is keep a few things in mind as you continue fighting for the things God has placed in your heart. Avoid some destructive mistakes that I've made in my own life.

I have spent a lot of years labeled as an extremist because of the way I fought for the needs of others. While I believe the passion in me might have been good, the lack of patience and kindness with those I was trying to pull in was destructive. I lost sight of God's desire for unity in His Bride, and that's no small sin. We have to figure out how to increase social action while growing in unity. Once we sacrifice one for the other, we lose our effectiveness and the right to be heard.

The church can sometimes feel like an emergency room. Every person who rushes into a hospital wants immediate help. Your broken arm hurts so bad that you barely notice the girl with the broken leg, the old man who just had a stroke, or the woman in labor. Patience is rare in an emergency room. Anger, tears, and frustration are not. Occasionally, arguments even break out as patients and families debate whose need is most urgent. It's not anyone's fault. We live in a world where devastating crises surround us.

One of the lessons I've learned in fighting for justice is that a lot of people are in need. Maybe Christians aren't quick to follow me at times because they are busy caring about equally important things. Consider the following list.

I hate labeling these "social issues" because we are talking about real suffering in real people and not "issues." Even as I wrote this, I was convicted that I hadn't given some of these things much thought lately. I was also grateful to God that some of you have been consistently fighting for these people.

Some Fight against Slavery/Human Trafficking

- 5 million children are in slavery right now. Many are forced into disgusting sexual acts multiple times a day.
- There are approximately 40 million slaves in the world today.

I can see why some of you are obsessed with freeing slaves. After all, we would all do anything in our power to rescue our own kids if they were trapped in that kind of horror.

Some Fight for Those Starving or Lacking Water

- 815 million people on the earth go hungry each day.
- 9 million people die every year of hunger-related causes.

Anyone who has fasted has felt the suffering of going a few days without food. Since Jesus said that neglecting the hungry was the same as neglecting Him, I can see why you keep this as top priority. If I saw Jesus starving, I'd probably drop everything to feed Him.

Some Fight for the Rights of the Unborn

- 3,000 unborn babies will be killed in the US today. Another 3,000 tomorrow …
- Worldwide, 50 million babies created in the image of God will die by abortion this year.

Is any sin worse than murder? I can see why some of you have devoted your lives to fighting for the unborn.

Some Fight for Widows and Orphans

- There are 150 million orphans in the world.
- There are 400,000 unwanted children in the US foster care system.
- In India alone there are 40 million widows, many suffering unspeakable atrocities.

Scripture explicitly explains that "religion that is pure and undefiled before God the Father is this: to visit orphans and widows in their affliction" (James 1:27). It makes sense that some of you would make this top priority. There are an estimated 400,000 Christian churches in the United States. That means we just need one more person per congregation to care!

Some Fight for the Unsaved

- 150,000 people die every day and face a Holy God who decides their eternal fate.

While some have changed their theology and are no longer burdened by this thought, others believe in both Heaven and Hell. Therefore, they can't imagine any cause ever being more important than the spread of the gospel, especially to those who have never heard of Jesus.

Just the Beginning

I haven't even begun to exhaust the list: the half million homeless in the United States, families of martyrs, believers in hostile countries being tortured as you read this because they refuse to deny Christ, people with special needs, wounded veterans, people with disabilities around the world treated like they are cursed, and the list goes on ... In fact, some people reading now are feeling offended because

I neglected to place their cause on the list. By the way, I didn't list these things in any particular order, so don't get offended by that either. We would all prioritize these differently. That's my point.

There are many tragedies on the earth right now. They must be fought against. When you look at the list, it's no wonder that every forty seconds, someone on this planet feels so hopeless that he or she commits suicide. Think about that for the next forty seconds.

We can't afford to discourage the passion of fellow believers. We are called to "stir up one another to love and good works" (Hebrews 10:24). So let's continue to lovingly challenge each other to greater depths of empathy and sacrifice. However, along the way, be careful not to become angry or frustrated with brothers and sisters who don't care as much as you do about a cause.

We live in a time when there is a lot to care about. God gifts people differently, and He stirs them up differently for the sake of different causes that are *all* on His heart. I may care about starving children more than you do. You may care about racial reconciliation more than I do. Someone else may care about the torture of Christians in persecuted countries more than we do. It doesn't mean we don't care. It's just that we will never all care equally. And unlike God, we only have so much capacity to take on action.

Unity requires a fight. It's also worth fighting for.

It will always be easier to seek out the people whose interests and affiliations most closely resemble your own—people whose life experiences resonate with yours and inform your choices and passions in similar ways. It will always be easier to write off those with whom your personality or opinions clash.

But there is something so beautiful and powerful about a group of incredibly diverse people uniting under a common banner. It shows the world that our common obsession with the worth of our King is more powerful than any social, political, culture, or economic divide. It shows them a picture of Heaven. Don't let your pride get in the way of that picture.

Fight through the Discouragement

As Christians, we didn't sign up for an easy life. Whatever attacks we endure as we seek to be faithful to Jesus—and it's always more sad when those attacks come from within the church—we can be sure that Christians throughout time have suffered far worse. It sometimes feels easier to throw up my hands, dismiss all the attackers, and let all the other Christians fend for themselves. Or to only invest myself in people who make my life easier. But that's not unity. It's impossible to be unified by yourself. I take courage in knowing that Jesus prayed that His followers would be unified and that He gave us the Holy Spirit to empower us for this. Unity requires a fight. It's also worth fighting for. Regardless of the opposition we face, we won't regret pursuing the clear commands of Jesus.

> *The end of all things is at hand; therefore be self-controlled and sober-minded for the sake of your prayers. Above all, keep loving one another earnestly, since love covers a multitude of sins. Show hospitality to one another without grumbling. As each has received a gift, use it to serve one another, as good stewards of God's varied grace: whoever speaks, as one who speaks oracles of God; whoever serves, as one who serves by the strength that God supplies—in order that in everything God may be glorified through Jesus Christ. To him belong glory and dominion forever and ever. Amen.*
>
> *Beloved, do not be surprised at the fiery trial when it comes upon you to test you, as though something strange were happening to you. But rejoice insofar as you share Christ's sufferings, that you may also rejoice and be glad when his glory is revealed.*
>
> —1 Peter 4:7–13

A Time to Move On

One of the things my old youth pastor said over and over was "move with the movers." In other words, don't get distracted by trying to convince everyone to follow. There will always be those who aren't interested, and you have to be willing to leave them behind. He would explain that Jesus didn't try to convince everyone but rather ended many of His messages with "he who has ears to hear, let him hear."

I now realize that this is exactly what has discouraged me from making any efforts toward unity. I've been aiming for 100 percent participation. It's never going to happen. Not everyone wants this. I kept trying to strategize on how I could get even the most arrogant separatists to join in the move toward unity. Because I used to be one of those who saw any ounce of ecumenicalism as heretical, I already knew the objections they would raise. I knew what they would say in their huddles as they belittled the heretics who wanted unity. They were the simpletons who didn't value theology and didn't know the Word like we did. They were the ignorant who wanted unity at the expense of truth. The more I thought about those who are stuck in this mentality, the more impossible the task seemed and the less inclined I was to try anything.

For the longest time, I wasn't willing to leave them behind. Maybe it was a loyalty I felt. Maybe it was because I kept thinking about what an asset they could be to the Body of Christ if they used their intelligence and passion to unite. Maybe I knew how they ridiculed others and didn't want to be on the receiving end of it. Whatever the reason, I wasn't able to let go until I saw that I had to choose between their divisive spirit or God's desire for unity.

It has only been recently that I have been able to let them go. I know what some of you are thinking: *"Isn't this a book on unity? How can you let go of a whole contingent of people who claim to know Jesus? How can you be loving them as you leave them behind?"* Sometimes it's necessary to run ahead in order to show people a glimpse of what is possible. As they see an example of unity and observe the blessings that God pours out on us, it may be the very thing that convinces them to reunite.

One of my favorite Bible stories is about Jonathan and his armor bearer (1 Samuel 14). Jonathan and his armor bearer decided to battle the entire Philistine army by themselves. All the other Hebrews were terrified, and many were hiding in the backwoods. God supernaturally blessed Jonathan, and suddenly he and his armor bearer were defeating a whole army. When Saul saw this, he took his men to join in the battle. Once they started chasing the Philistines away, then the last group of Hebrews finally joined the chase.

We can't wait until everyone agrees to join the fight for unity. As God blesses the faith of the few, others will join.

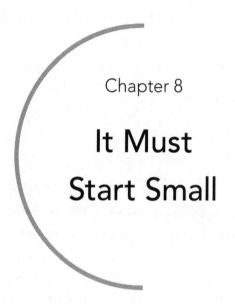

Chapter 8

It Must
Start Small

From the Invisible to the Most Visible

One of the mistakes I see time and time again in the pursuit of unity (among other pursuits) is that everyone wants to jump to the macro-scale. I am sure that many of these people have good intentions. They want to get the message to as many people as possible; they want to see revival.

But all too often, the message to the masses is robbed of its power because it's not accompanied by a life that reflects its power. So if you feel passionate about seeing greater unity in the church, I would urge you to start small. Get your life in order before making speeches.

Start with just you and God. Spend time marveling at the mystery of oneness with God and repenting of pride and divisiveness. Learn what it means to *abide* in the Father, because apart from Him you will not bear fruit (John 15:4–5). Ask Him to help you see the people around you through His eyes. I've heard a friend, who is another well-known Christian leader, talk about a time he was flipping through *Charisma* magazine, looking at the pictures of other pastors and leaders. He confessed feeling indifferent toward each person and told how he started begging God to let him see each person the way He sees them. My friend was convinced that God has called us to so much more than just indifference toward our brothers and sisters in Christ. He refused to put the magazine down until he felt God's love for them. The absence of bitterness was not enough. God commanded us to love them as He loved us. Follow my friend's example: confess your shortcomings and beg God to change your heart.

Examine your marriage: you can't start a movement toward unity while you're getting a divorce. Are you truly one with your spouse? Are you loving your wife and laying your life down for her as Christ did for the Church? Are you honoring your husband as unto Christ? If we cannot lovingly work through conflict in a context as intimate and committed as marriage, we can hardly expect to be able to do so in our churches. "For if someone does not know how to manage his own household, how will he care for God's church?" (1 Timothy 3:5).

Think about your specific church family. Don't be quick to lament disunity in the American church or the global church while you're unkind, dismissive, and loveless toward the people in your own church Body. Dietrich Bonhoeffer warned about the difference between loving the *concept* of a united community versus loving the *people* who are actually in our community:

> Every human wish dream that is injected into the Christian community is a hindrance to genuine community and must be banished if genuine community is to survive. He who loves his dream of a community more than the Christian community itself becomes a destroyer of the latter, even though his personal intentions may be ever so honest and earnest and sacrificial.[7]

He's saying that it's dangerous to hold some ideal about living in a united community that's nothing more than a daydream. What we need instead is to love the actual people who stand before us and to find unity with those specific

God didn't call us to neutrality. He wants every word to be spoken in love.

people. If we can't find unity there, we can't find meaningful unity at all.

God didn't call us to neutrality. He wants every word to be spoken in love. Every sentence at every level of interaction should be spoken in love, leading to greater unity. If you could get a transcript of your last conversation, how many sentences would have been spoken to promote love and unity?

The Poison of Selfish Ambition

James 3 warns us that "where jealousy and selfish ambition exist, there will be disorder and every vile practice" (v. 16). Selfish ambition is rarely spoken about. It's become accepted, assumed, and even praised at times. God recently showed me how selfish ambition has been somewhat regular in my life. He showed me times when I started out pure but then selfish ambition crept in. He showed me how the prophets didn't have lofty goals like "I'm going to lead the masses" but strove only to be faithful to whatever God called them to. Think of Isaiah, Jeremiah, Ezekiel, and the others: their ambition was to follow directions.

Are we sure that goal setting and ten-year plans are biblical? It's curious that every young minister has a vision or an ambition to lead masses in revival. How much of that ambition is selfish? Is it just coincidental that leading a great revival would also be the most enjoyable lifestyle for all of us? It's rare to meet people who have the ambition to be hated and mistreated like Christ or the prophets. It's rare to find someone whose ambition is to suffer and die like the apostles.

I want to see repentance and revival as much as anyone. I just want to make sure I'm following God and not selfish ambition. As I look back in life, I see a good percentage of Kingdom-focused motives mixed in with some selfish ambition. That's not okay because the James passage says that where selfish ambition even "exists," it will lead to disorder. Everyone knows the Christian world is in chaos. I believe that's because of the amount of selfish ambition in the leadership.

Our evangelical tradition gives freedom to every individual Christian leader to express his or her interpretation of Scripture without accountability, so we take full advantage of that. Christians in the United States spend far more time criticizing others than sharing the gospel. New blogs, podcasts, and websites are created daily. These often lead to new churches and even denominations. It's for this reason that thousands of Christian denominations exist, each believing it is the most biblically accurate.

We also live in a time when people are hungry for readership and listeners. Some pastors have realized that if they make a video titled *The Glory of Christ*, they may get a hundred views, but *Francis Chan Denies Jesus* is sure to get thousands. So we grow our base of followers however we can without considering how this appears to a dying world, to say nothing of what it does to the heart of God.

Just after the passage quoted above, James writes "What causes quarrels and what causes fights among you? Is it not this, that your passions are at war within you?" (4:1). As soon as we begin to mix Kingdom objectives with selfish ones, we are undermining our own efforts, because we will reap what we sow.

The Danger of Denominations

When you consider all the divisions that have fractured the church into literally thousands of branches, it's hard to believe that we all claim to follow the same Jesus who prayed before He died that we would all be one as He and the Father are one. It's especially striking when you examine the reasons for some of the major rifts. For example, the famous split of 1054 mentioned earlier happened when the Western Catholic Church and Eastern Orthodox Church could not agree on whether the Holy Spirit proceeds from the Father only (the Eastern Church's view) or from the Father *and the Son* (the Western Church's addition to the established creed). The debate was over a single Latin word: *filioque* ("and from the Son"). They excommunicated each other and created a rift that hasn't been healed for almost a thousand years. So many subsequent battles and executions and divides have continued in the Body of Christ.

I'm not saying that some of these splits didn't arise from genuine movements of God's Spirit. I am grateful for many of the insights that came about during the Protestant Reformation, which began in 1517. Martin Luther wrestled to interpret Scripture accurately and stood against many of the abuses in the Catholic Church at that time regarding the gospel and justification. I want to have his boldness and conviction regarding what the Scriptures actually say. But most of us have never heard Luther's warning to his fellow reformer, Melanchthon: "After our death, there will rise many harsh and terrible sects. God help us!"

About 300 years after the Reformation and about 175 years ago, the Protestant church historian Philip Schaff described his cultural moment like this: "[The sect system is a] grand disease which has fastened itself upon the heart of Protestantism, and which must be considered ... more dangerous, because it appears ordinarily in the imposing garb of piety."[8]

I'm struck by how well his words describe what we're still experiencing today. Schaff was writing with regard to the Reformation, but as I've said, the issue is much older than that. For hundreds of years, our propensity to divide and attack—to form sects—has been eating us alive. Paul warned us: "If you bite and devour one another, watch out that you are not consumed by one another" (Gal. 5:15). But we don't seem to have ever taken his words seriously.

Often, our divisions come when we disagree about the right way to interpret the Bible. This was certainly the case with Luther's Reformation. But Schaff points out a reality that is still true today: many times huge divisions come between people who can sign the same doctrinal statement but can't agree on the same methodology. He said the disagreements in his day "turn not so much on doctrine, as on the constitution and forms of the Church. In place of schools and systems we have parties and sects, which in many cases appear in full inexorable opposition, even while occupying the platform of the very same confession."

This continues to be true. Churches and groups with nearly identical statements of faith find it impossible to validate what God is doing among a neighboring church or group.

From his vantage point in 1845, Schaff foresaw this trajectory would lead us into dangerous places: "Where the process of separation is destined to end, no human calculation can foretell. Anyone who has ... some inward experience and a ready tongue may persuade himself that he is called to be a reformer;... in his spiritual vanity and pride [he causes] a revolutionary rupture with the historical life of the Church, to which he holds himself immeasurably superior. He builds himself of a night accordingly a new chapel, in which now for

I have been praying that God's people could recover the love and unity that the Bible consistently emphasizes.

the first time since the age of the apostles a pure congregation is to be formed; baptizes his followers with his own name …"

Those are strong words. But was he wrong? Have we not seen this happen time and again on large and small scales? Schaff's words are harsh, but I think he's right: "Thus the deceived multitude … is converted not to Christ and his truth, but to the arbitrary fancies and baseless opinions of an individual.… What is built is no Church, but a chapel, to whose erection Satan himself has made the most liberal contribution."

Leaving room for a genuine work of the Spirit from time to time, I think we need to hear Schaff's strong language. Do we think God is pleased with our constant excommunications and "farewells"?

For every denomination that has split off, how many individual Christians have also formed their own divisions? All our separations continue to speed up—where will this all end?

My prayer in writing this book has been that we as a church could come to our senses and see all of the division and infighting as something contrary to God's design. I have been praying that God's people could recover the love and unity that the Bible consistently emphasizes. I have been asking God to create an army of people who believe we can be united in the love of Jesus through the empowerment of the Spirit.

I know this won't happen because I've asked us to do it. I know it won't happen in response to all of us trying harder to get along. But I believe the Spirit of God can unite us in ways that are supernatural. I believe He wants to do this. I believe God has told us that this is what He wants to do in His church. So I believe this will happen. We've gotten pretty far offtrack, but God is constantly pursuing His wayward sheep.

Lead the Revolution

What comes to mind when you hear the phrase "powerful Christian leader"? Most of us would envision a person standing on a stage speaking to thousands of people and mobilizing them toward some large-scale action. Others may be thinking of someone with an online presence that draws millions of followers. Consider the apostle Paul, who certainly influenced his generation but has impacted millions and millions over the past two thousand years. People are still reading Paul's writings and admiring his example.

> But we were gentle among you, like a nursing
> mother taking care of her own children. So,
> being affectionately desirous of you, we were
> ready to share with you not only the gospel of

God but also our own selves, because you had
become very dear to us.

—1 Thessalonians 2:7–8

Sometimes it's easy to forget that Paul did not spend his days standing in front of coliseums filled with people. Instead, he cared for people deeply. He went from place to place loving people deeply and sharing his life with them. Perhaps no one writing or reading this book will have the kind of lasting impact Paul has had, but maybe we would if we followed his example. It's usually the people who aren't thinking about the masses who actually reach the masses. They are just busy loving the people God places before them. As love prompts unusual acts of sacrifice, their examples become remembered by the masses. Most of the voices we hear today will be silenced at death because they had no loving actions to be remembered.

Little children, let us not love in word or talk
but in deed and in truth.

—1 John 3:18

My friend John is an older man whose wife died tragically. In addition to losing his sight, diabetes had destroyed both of his kidneys. With his wife gone, he had no one to take him to dialysis treatments. An announcement was made to the church that John needed help. My friend Keith offered to drive him even though it would take a lot of hours out of his schedule. Though he worked a full-time job and had two children at home, he wanted to serve this brother in Christ whom he hardly knew. The first time they went to the hospital, Keith was lost and his new blind friend wasn't much help. It gave them time to laugh, talk, and get to know each other. As John shared his story and explained his medical condition, Keith grew in love for John. He was so moved that a few weeks later he donated one of his kidneys to him!

Living in Hong Kong, I've had the pleasure of spending time with my friend Jackie. She is one of my heroes. At age twenty-two, she boarded a boat in England that took her to Hong Kong. She arrived in 1966 with ten dollars, and she lives there to this day. She started ministering to drug addicts in the most dangerous part of the city and hasn't stopped. Though she is seventy-six, I have a hard time keeping up with the schedule she keeps. I love this woman! We have theological and practical differences, but it matters so little to me. She is an example to me. Her commitment to Christ and love for people are clear signs that she too is a recipient of God's grace. Anyone who knows Jackie knows that she cringes whenever any attention is given to her. She wants all glory to go to the One who gave her grace to serve Him all these years.

Unity is difficult when all we do is talk. The early church produced the book of Acts; the modern church produced a book of Talks. Their leaders died living out the gospel; we make a living by talking about it. The more we bear fruit, the easier unity will be. When we begin to see one another conforming our actions and lifestyles to those of Jesus and the early church, we will be more prone to unite. It will become a joy and an honor to serve alongside such men and women. They may not come from your denomination or theological background, but you can celebrate as they give glory to Jesus.

Conclusion:
A Return to
Childlike Faith

"For we must all appear before the judgment seat of Christ, so that each one may receive what is due for what he has done in the body, whether good or evil."

2 Corinthians 5:10

The older I get, the less I think about what others have said about me and the more I think about what Jesus will say to me. Before I wrote this paragraph, I spent an hour imagining what it will be like when I see God. This has been a healthy practice in my life, and I need to do it more often. As

I pictured bowing before Him, I thought about the regrets I will have about my time on earth. I am aware of so many failures, and many more will be exposed on that Day. Only then will I discover how much my pride and self-centeredness hurt other people, and the church at large.

I tried to write this book with only that Day in mind. What will I regret saying or not saying? On that Day, I won't have even an ounce of concern about what others think of me. I will stand before my Maker and answer for my life. As I look back on fifty-three years of failures, I know of things I have done that hurt the Church. I also know of things I failed to do, which also hurt the Church. I know better than to wallow in the shame of past failures. At the same time, I don't want to create new regrets for the future.

Take some time to consider what will matter to you on that Final Day. It is so healthy to take your eyes off everything you see now (2 Cor. 4:18). Just picture standing or laying prostrate before a Holy God in the end. This is what motivates me to make some of the hardest decisions in my life.

Some of you need to distance yourselves from those who are leading you to divide from brothers and sisters in Christ. Others need to embrace those you have wrongfully divided from. May the Holy Spirit give you the necessary courage and humility. Remember to not get overwhelmed with all the division throughout the world. Whom do you personally need to have a conversation with? You don't want to be

We were created for unity, saved to be unified, and will spend eternity worshipping as one Body.

embracing the divisive, nor be distancing yourself from true children of God, on that Day. We want Him to find us desperately pursuing the unity He commanded.

Be Mature Enough to Worship like a Child

By the grace of God, I still have a childlike faith that the Body of Christ can unite during my lifetime. I may be crazy but as the world gets more divided, I actually believe this is the exact time that God wants to unite His Kingdom. I keep imagining how happy we will be as we start coming together. It's what we want. We were created for unity, saved to be unified, and will spend eternity worshipping as one Body. Some may view me as immature for believing that deeper worship will unite us. I think I am finally mature enough to believe like a child. His Spirit pushes us into a deep worship that unites us. The Spirit-filled believer will not allow anything to break his or her participation in this ongoing, unified worship service.

> *And do not get drunk with wine, for that is debauchery, but be filled with the Spirit, addressing one another in psalms and hymns and spiritual songs, singing and making melody to the Lord with your heart, giving thanks*

always and for everything to God the Father in
the name of our Lord Jesus Christ, submitting
to one another out of reverence for Christ.
—Ephesians 5:18–21

Spirit-filled people will not allow conflicts to keep them from addressing each other with "psalms and hymns and spiritual songs." Mature people aren't so easily diverted from praise.

Spirit-filled people are constantly "singing and making melody to the Lord." This is an unbroken worship that comes from "your heart." You don't require others to pull you into worship. The Spirit stirs you from within as songs and melodies come out.

Spirit-filled people are "giving thanks always and for everything." Thanksgiving can't be stopped in the life of a godly follower. Even trials and suffering can lead to thanksgiving for the person who is walking in the Spirit.

Spirit-filled people have a "reverence for Christ." A fear of God leads to "submitting to one another." We are unable to just think about ourselves. His Spirit leads us to consider the importance of others.

According to this biblical definition of being Spirit-filled, could you describe yourself as being a Spirit-filled person?

Is it really as simple as becoming Spirit-filled? Would this really fix every Christian conflict? Yes.

Just as no Spirit-filled couple has ever divorced, no Spirit-filled church can split. It is only when we stop addressing each other with psalms, stop singing to the Lord from our hearts, stop thanking God for everything, and stop submitting to one another out of reverence for Christ that we are able to divide from one another. If you think I'm wrong, ask yourself if you have ever seen it happen. How many people do you know who live out even one of those Spirit-filled traits?

Right now, I'm thinking of two women: Joni and Susan. They are two of the most Spirit-filled people I know. They have been examples to me of people who seem like they literally never stop praising and thanking Him. I don't think they've ever met, but I can only imagine watching them meet and having sweet fellowship in the presence of Jesus. As they take turns boasting in the Lord, I can't imagine them ever discovering something worth dividing over. They both love sitting right at the Lord's feet too much. Neither could bear walking away.

Let's end this book the way we started it: praise Him.

> Lord, I praise you because I exist. I love being alive, and I am so humbled to be created in Your image. You made me in such a way that I can become one with You now. You accomplished this by the death of Your Son on the cross. His blood has cleansed me. Worthy is the

Lamb who was slain! You have adopted me, and I love being Your child. I am overwhelmed by the fact that You desire me. I want to be one with You far more than I want anything.

Please cleanse me of my pride, selfish ambition, and self-centeredness. You want me to be perfectly one with all my brothers and sisters in Christ. I want this too. Lord, increase this desire in me and in all Your children. I am sorry for all I have done that has caused division. I am sorry for all I have not done, allowing these divisions to continue. Increase my love for Your children. Almighty God, unite us by Your glory and for the sake of Your glory. I long to see Your Son's prayer answered—that we would become perfectly one, just as You and Jesus are one. My soul longs for perfect unity in Your presence forever.

Praise Father, Son, and Holy Spirit.

Amen.

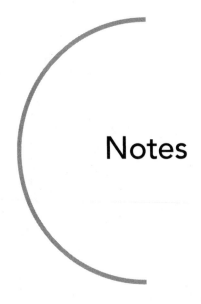

Notes

1. A. W. Tozer in John Snyder, *Behold Your God: Rethinking God Biblically*, (New Albany, MS: Media Gratiae, 2013), 15.

2. "Most American Christians Do Not Believe that Satan or the Holy Spirit Exist," Barna, April 13, 2009, www.barna.com/research/most-american-christians-do-not-believe-that-satan-or-the-holy-spirit-exist/.

3. John Snyder, *Behold Your God: Rethinking God Biblically*, (New Albany, MS: Media Gratiae, 2013), 125.

4. Matthew 6:10, King James Version (Public Domain).

5. Watchman Nee, *The Normal Christian Church Life*, (Anaheim, CA: Living Stream Ministry, 2005), 48.

6. JAY-Z, vocalist, "Streets Is Watching" by Labi Siffre, Ski Beatz, and JAY-Z, track 5 on *In My Lifetime, Vol. 1*, , Def Jam Recordings and Roc-a-Fella Records, 1997.

7. Dietrich Bonhoeffer, *Life Together*, trans. John W. Doberstien (London: SCM Press, 1954), Kindle loc. 164 or 1473.

8. Philip Schaff, *The Principle of Protestantism as Related to the Present State of the Church*, trans. John W. Nevin (Chambersburg: German Reformed Church, 1845). Quotations in this section are pulled from pages 107–116.

Scripture Index

Scriptures are listed in the order in which they appear.

Epigraph

Ephesians 4:11–16   7

Introduction

Psalm 103:1   14
Romans 5:10–11   15
Ephesians 2:3–4   15
Romans 3:23–25   15
1 John 3:1   15
2 Corinthians 5:21   15
John 14:21–23   15
Romans 13:8   16
Isaiah 66:1–2   17

Proverbs 6:16–19   18
John 17:20–23   20
Ephesians 4:1–6   20
Titus 3:9–11   20
Galatians 3:27–28   21
Romans 14:4   21
1 Corinthians 1:10   21
Philippians 2:1–2   21
Colossians 2:16–19   22
1 Thessalonians 3:11–13   22
1 Timothy 1:5–7   23
1 Timothy 6:3–5   23
2 Timothy 2:23–25   23

James 3:17–18	24
1 John 2:9–11	24
1 John 4:10–12	24
Matthew 5:9	25
John 15:18	26
Philippians 1:27–28	28
Galatians 5:19–23	29
Galatians 5:22–23	30
Matthew 12:34	30
James 4	31
James 3	31
Mark 12:28–31	32
Colossians 3:12–15	33
John 17	33

Chapter 1: It's What the Trinity Wants

Genesis 1:26	35
Genesis 1:2	36
John 1:1–3	36
James 3:8–10	36
John 4:24	37
John 14–17	37
John 14:9	37
John 14:16–17	37
John 14:23	38
John 15:4	38
John 17:20–23	38
1 Timothy 6:16	39
Ephesians 3:19	39
2 Peter 1:4	39
Exodus 16:16–19	39
2 Corinthians 5:17	39
James 4:5	41
Proverbs 6:16–19	42
Romans 14:15	44

Ephesians 2:13–22	45
Revelation 5:12	45
Revelation 4:5	47
Ephesians 4:30	47
Ephesians 4:29–31	47
Ezekiel 9:4	49
Revelation 9:4	49
Ezekiel 9:4–6	50
2 Peter 2:7–8	51
Ezekiel 21:6	51
Zephaniah 3:18	51
Revelation 2:2–6	51
Nehemiah 1:4; 2:2–3	51
Psalm 119:136	51
Jonah 4:10–11	52
Amos 6:4–6	52

Chapter 2: It's What You Want

Ephesians 1:19–23	54
Romans 8:11–14	55
2 Peter 1:4	55
1 Corinthians 11:18–19	56
1 John 2:19	57
1 John 1:6	57
1 John 2:3–6	57
1 John 2:9–10	58
1 John 3:6, 10	58
1 John 3:14–15	58
1 John 3:17–18	58
1 John 4:7–8	59
1 John 4:19–21	59
1 John 5:2–3	59
1 John 1:3	61
Revelation 3:20	62
1 John 5:13	62

Revelation 3   63, 64
2 Corinthians 6:14   64
Romans 12:1   65
Luke 18   66
Luke 19   68
Luke 9:23–24   70
Luke 9:57–62   70
Luke 14:25–33   71
John 10:3–5   73
Acts 4:32–35   73

Chapter 3: It's What the World Needs

Revelation 20:11–15   77
2 Thessalonians 1:6–10   78
2 Corinthians 5:10–11   79
Philippians 1:27–28   79
Philippians 1:15–18   82
1 Samuel 13   83
1 Samuel 10–11   83
1 Samuel 15   84
Hebrews 11:6   88
John 17:20–23   89
Colossians 1:19   89
1 Corinthians 12:14–26   95
John 17   95
1 Corinthians 12   95

Chapter 4: It Starts with Repentance

Psalm 139:23–24   98
1 Corinthians 14:39   100
1 Corinthians 13:12   102
1 Corinthians 2   103
1 Corinthians 1   104
1 Corinthians 13:8–12   104
Isaiah 55:8–9   107
1 Corinthians 3   110
1 Corinthians 6   110
1 Corinthians 7   110
1 Corinthians 8   110
1 Corinthians 11   110
1 Corinthians 12   110
1 Corinthians 13–14   111
1 Corinthians 3:1–17   111
1 Corinthians 3:21   112
1 Corinthians 4:3–5   112
Galatians 1:10   114
1 Corinthians 1:10–13   115
1 Corinthians 1:29   115
1 Corinthians 1:31   115
Matthew 6:10   117

Chapter 5: It Comes with Maturity

Ephesians 4:11–16   120
Colossians 1:28–29   121
James 1:4   121
2 Peter 1:5–7   121
Galatians 5:22–23   121
Colossians 3:12–14   122
Hebrews 5:12   125
1 Corinthians 8:1   125
James 4:6   126
2 Peter 3:18   126
Matthew 23   127
2 Timothy 4:2   130
John 13:34–35   132
1 Thessalonians 3:11–13   133
1 Thessalonians 4:9–10   134
2 Thessalonians 1:3   134
Luke 14:26   135

Matthew 12:46–50   135
Matthew 22:36–40   135
1 Corinthians 13:6   136
Matthew 7:14   136

Chapter 6: It Survives with Love

John 1:47   142
Psalm 133:1, 3   144
Galatians 1:8   145
1 Corinthians 15:1–8   145
2 John 7–11   146
1 Corinthians 2:2   147
Matthew 24:5   147
1 Corinthians 12:3   147
Colossians 2:16–23   147
1 Timothy 1:4   147
1 Timothy 4:3   148
2 Timothy 4:4   148
1 John 4:1–3   148
2 John 7   148
Jude 4   148
Galatians 2:11–14   148
Romans 14:5   149
Romans 14:13–19   150
Ephesians 4:1–3   153
Acts 10–11   155
Acts 11:18   155
Luke 15:11–32   157
1 John   159

Chapter 7: It Requires a Fight

Matthew 5:9   161
Matthew 23:23–24   162

1 Corinthians 5:11–13   164
1 Corinthians 4:5   164
Matthew 7:1–2   164
Matthew 18:15–20   165
1 Corinthians 5:4–5   165
2 Corinthians 1:9   168
Luke 6:28   173
Matthew 5:44–47   173
Titus 3:10   175
James 3:2   176
Psalm 34:1   176
Philippians 4:8   176
Luke 18:9–14   176
James 1:27   182
Hebrews 10:24   185
1 Peter 4:7–13   187
1 Samuel 14   189

Chapter 8: It Must Start Small

John 15:4–5   192
1 Timothy 3:5   193
James 3:16   194
James 4:1   197
Galatians 5:15   199
1 Thessalonians 2:7–8   203
1 John 3:18   203

Conclusion: A Return to Childlike Faith

2 Corinthians 5:10   207
2 Corinthians 4:18   208
Ephesians 5:18–21   211

Coming Fall 2021

Until Unity Community Study Guide and Videos

More information at
untilunitybook.com

For your church.
For your small group.
For you.

Discover why so many have been impacted by
the challenging message of Francis Chan.

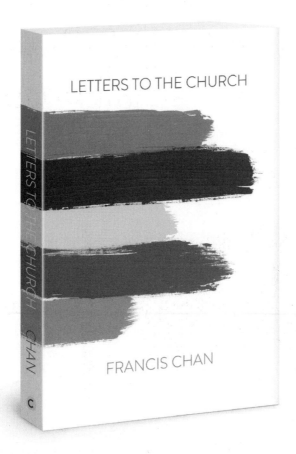

IT'S TIME TO
RETHINK CHURCH

If all you had to reference was the Bible,
what would Church look like?